A Handful of
Seashells

A Handful of Seashells

Seashells

M J Harper

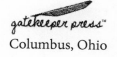
gatekeeper press™
Columbus, Ohio

A Handful of Seashells
Published by Gatekeeper Press
2167 Stringtown Rd, Suite 109
Columbus, OH 43123-2989
www.GatekeeperPress.com

Copyright © 2021 by M J Harper

Library of Congress Control Number: 2021949623

ISBN (paperback): 9781662914492
eISBN: 9781662914508

Contents

Acknowledgments

This collection of stories revolve around lived experiences most of them my own. Set in the sleepy Archipelago of the Bay Islands, the Western Caribbean and *La Mosquitia* where I have lived for most of my adult life enjoying mixed fortunes, sadness and joy. The one constant has been the kindness of the Islanders who would give you the shirt off their backs to help. When I arrived to these shores in the second half of the 80's it was as an English Teacher at a village school where I was introduced to the simple yet idyllic Island lifestyle in the tiny island of St. Helene. The islanders were patient with me and took their time to teach me much as I was teaching them, for this I will always be grateful to Dave Bowman and Eddy Pandy, Wilson and Woudsin Bodden, David and Johnny Warren and those no longer with us Walney Bodden, Iverson Bodden, Uncle James Bodden, Ulrich Adolf, Roland Matute. Were it not for the love and support of my former wife, Carolyn and her family I probably wouldn't have ended up making my home here. In the pre-development boom in the Bay Islands in the late 80's early 90's there was no willful employment if it wasn't related to the fishing industry and through my friendship with Anne Jennings and her husband Mike Brown I was given a house to look after while I worked as a welder, carpenter, mechanic, fisherman and diver. Both are now deceased but I treasure my moments with them both talking literature and doing the Times crossword. I owe a debt of gratitude to Harvey and Ginnie Mayer (both deceased), Virginia Castillo, Marion Seaman, Averyl Muller, Leeker McNab (deceased), Crellin Kaighen, Richard and Jenny McNab, Randy French (deceased), Richard and Betsy Watson, Jim and Julia Rukin, Brian and Lisa Blanchard, Harvey McNab, Murvin and Lurleene McNab, Anna Pandy (deceased), Bill and Lulu Pandy (both deceased), Oswald Ebanks (deceased), Capt. Lem Ebanks (deceased), Ione Miller and Goldie Cooper (deceased) all of whom shared kindnesses to me and my young family at that time unselfishly and who helped me along as I followed a path I never Imagined I would have ever taken.

I must thank my artist brother Joe Harper who willingly volunteered to paint the cover picture from a photograph by Tom Leopold (a sometime resident of St. Helene) There is more to tell and more people to whom I must express my gratitude but that is for another book, another collection of stories, another handful of seashells.

For J.P 'Pete' Traskey
Who instilled in me an appreciation of Literature

The Dragon

A simple life it was then. A supper of fried fish, red beans, and coconut bread with a cup of fever grass tea around 6:00 in the evening and then half an hour of the BBC World Service, as long as I had batteries. At about 7:00 my eyelids would become heavy, and I'd drift off with the trade winds lulling me to sleep through the open shutters of our little shack. Made of board and resting on oak posts, it had been a small store of sorts that once sold the basics—rice, beans, flour, and on Fridays, chicken. There was no electricity and so the freezer was an old kerosene wick job which did well enough. By the time we got married the store had gone in the hole, mainly because the extended family had kicked the credit can too far down the road.

Every other day I would go diving, alternating with fishing or working on my small plantation where I had some cassava and plantain suckers taking their time growing while I constantly fought the cutter ants. On diving days, I would get up at 4:00 and wake my wife, who would draw me a cup of strong coffee through a linen bag and set me a piece of heavy flour cake ("sinker," we called it) on a saucer to eat. After this I would smoke the first cigarette of the day and place four more inside a small plastic bag that I would tie thoroughly to keep them dry. I kept the plastic bag underneath my hat or in the very bow of the dory under the plywood cap. I would take only four (they cost ten-centavos lempira then) which was what I could afford, unless of course I hit luck while diving and had enough to have a few beers of a weekend, and then I'd buy a whole packet. I planned ahead of time how I would smoke the four cigarettes; the first when I had finished the hour-long paddle up to the cays, the second around mid-morning when I felt the first hunger pangs, the third when I made ready to paddle back down to leeward, and the last when I was halfway down, which was mostly when I was abreast of Hog Reef. After this first smoke before dawn, I would rack up my diving equipment. It was free diving, mind you, no tanks, so I would just take a mask ("diving face," as the Helene boys would whimsically refer to it) and snorkel, my heavy fins ("flappers"), a hookstick for the lobsters, and my Italian speargun that cost me a hundred lempiras at carnival time in La Ceiba, for any fish I would come across.

I had my hands and my lungs for the conchs. After several months of freediving with the Helene men, I had learned to hyperventilate slowly before making my dive and effectively clearing my ears on the way down. Once down there, I knew how to move slowly enough to conserve my air. I was able to get down to ten fathoms at times and bring up two broadleaf conchs. My proudest moment to date had been the day I was diving ship channel and from above noticed four long whips of two big lobsters underneath a pot loaf rock at about eight fathoms. It was a calm day with little current and the water was clear. I took two deep breaths, as much as my lungs would hold, let go of the dory rope (I was diving alone that day), and tilted my body downward on the third , letting the weight of my perpendicular trunk and kicking legs taking me down. Halfway down I forced a yawn with my mouth closed, which always worked for me to equalize. When I got level with the small cave in the rock where the bugs were, I positioned my hook under the chest of the biggest one and hooked up, the wounded lobster croaking and flipping its tail. Controlling my urge to panic and go to the surface with my lungs reaching the bursting point, I stabbed the lobster's chest with the pointed end of my hookstick and killed it to stop it wriggling. I took it off the hook and gaffed the second one. With it on the hook, croaking, I made my escape to the surface, kicking as fast as my fins would push me upwards. When I broke the surface, it was up to my navel, and I thought I would dislocate my jawbone opening my mouth that wide to inhale the sweet fresh air!

I would place my pitiful array of kit neatly in the dory head because space was limited. The only other features in the dory were a movable seat or "thwart" (pronounced *tort*) and a bailer that more often than not was a cut-in-half and hollowed-out Calabash nut used to bail out all the water that either seeped in or came in on my cut-off jeans every time I returned from a stint in the water. The dory itself was a ten-by-two-foot dug-out canoe. The wood was mahogany and was reportedly twenty years old. It belonged to my father-in-law who charged me no rent for its use except the simple levy of one fish per trip. But it couldn't be just any fish. Before I knew the old man's ways, on sparse days I would take a "squab" or a "gilumbo" or an "old shoe," but he would have none of it and would let me know that I had to bring a snapper or a jack at least. He'd keep a check of it in his head and some days I would end up owing him four or five fish. The dory was known in the yard as *The Dragon* and was about as obstinate as its owner, God rest his soul. It was called so because it had developed a split in the bow over the years that looked like a mouth. It was a difficult dory to paddle, and as the day wore on it would become more and more stubborn, as if it had a temperament of its own. I would steer it to port, and it would want to veer to starboard. The good thing about *The Dragon* was that it wasn't cranky, and I could even stand up in it to better survey the reef as I looked for my special rocks.

I would be at the Cays or Barbarat by 6:00 with the sun just getting stronger on the eastern horizon and the reef and the banks turning blue from black. I had only learned to handle a dory a year earlier and although I was "the toughest white man ever to have lived on Helene" (a compliment I reveled in), I still couldn't paddle as fast as the others. The Helene boys had been paddling around in dories along the reef and in open water since they were toddlers. When I had some money, I would buy my own dory.

On my way "up the line to windward" I would sing old songs I could only remember fragments of. I would remember bits of my childhood and my adolescence. I would laugh to myself at jokes that I had heard years ago, and I would plan in my head what I would do on the island, how I would build my house right down to the finest detail, and what I would try to grow in my plantation. I would consider myself and my standing amongst the islanders; I had married one of them and she was four months pregnant. Her family and friends had welcomed me and taught me the skills I needed to be able to survive and eke out a living. They seemed to like me, but by the same token every time I came back from diving, I detected quizzical looks on their faces as if to say, "He'll soon snap out of it but we'll humour him for the time being." A few of them had gone so far as to ask me why I had not moved out to Oakridge or French Harbour to look for "real" work at the packing plants. My wife nagged me a little, but her mother nagged quite a bit more on the subject and more frequently since the belly had started to show. As they saw it, it would be better all-around if I worked for a steady wage rather than "killing myself" diving. "Look at ya, yer all *mauger* and your hair getting red, man, *chah*!"

The fact of the matter was that we weren't starving, and I enjoyed the sun and the sea and the colours of the reef and the satisfying primal thrill that hunting to survive afforded me. I enjoyed being respected amongst the islanders for being a good diver, a deep diver, despite not being one of them. Granted, I'd had some setbacks, like when *The Dragon* hauled me across the patchy reef in a hard squall in July and ripped my legs to shreds, which then became infected. I was off diving for two weeks while I recovered, dreading the thought of developing gangrene, but the mother-in-law who despised me nursed my wounds back with *Larry Weed* and *Bittercup Bark* just so she could bring it up later in any argument. I had always been bothered by an uneasy feeling that my wife's attraction to me was driven more by her mother's ambitions than her own affections. I saw her as distant and indifferent with me and often felt like asking her if she would have been happier shacked up with a local boy instead. My mother-in-law was astute and treated me like a king before our hurried marriage, but when she discovered that I wasn't going to take her daughter away from the island to my country, things soured and she changed.

On this particular day, I had woken my wife up to draw the coffee and get me the cake, and she started mumbling something into the pillow that I couldn't quite catch, but it sounded negative. I was on edge that day. Money was tight and, as I did at times, I resorted to feeling sorry for myself and being petty to gain a little attention. "I bet you'll be sorry you didn't get up and get my breakfast if I disappear today, eaten by a shark!" I didn't wait for the coffee and grabbed my piece of sinker and my gallon of water and headed out to the dock to rack up the diving things.

This same day I had in mind diving Yankee Joe Reef (called Revolution Reef on the charts). it was flat calm. The sea was like glass, so I could look around the crab holes for lobster and maybe, as was common on this patch, I would run into a mutton snapper I could strike at. After this my plan, subject to change as always, was to paddle down to the reef in Pascual Bight off Barbarat and see how the pickings were down there. It was November and we were always expectant of the northers; in the yard the night before, we'd gathered around the transistor listening to Radio Belize out of Belize City before it moved to Belmopan and we lost the signal. You must remember, there was no electricity at that time and no television. Our only link to the world outside the island was a battery-powered radio. The forecast was for calm seas but within twenty-four hours a strong cold front was heading into the Western Caribbean. I knew I had time to be back by 4:00 before the west wind made down, which was the first sign of the norther bearing down.

There was a slight chill at that hour and the Milky Way above in all its splendour filled me with the feeling that I was the only person on Earth and the show of stars above was for me alone. "All the bright company of Heaven... Orion`s belt and sworded hip," as Julian Grenfell had put it back during the Great War. As I eased away from the dock, I could make out another dark shape moving along the water from the west. It was probably Sam Warren from Bentley Bay. I could see by the way he was paddling—long, even strokes with his head kicking back slightly as he dug into the water.

I made quick time. *The Dragon* was cooperating and I was abreast of the little cay when a sliver of sun began to peer over the eastern horizon just to the south of Bonacca. I had amused myself by remembering in minute detail the last game of rugby I ever played, and as a consequence the journey east flew by. Our team had been so much smaller than our opponents, having in their pack some huge Nigerians with legs like tree trunks. We were down twelve to nothing by half-time but through sheer doggedness, courage, and camaraderie we were able to come back and win by three points. I remembered the smell of the wintergreen, the rattle of studs on the changing room floor, and the pressure of the tape around my head to hold my ears back in the scrum, a pleasing moment that I always looked back on. I was at Yankee Joe Reef a while after dawn, smoked the long-anticipated cigarette, and threw the painter in the water so that I could tow *The Dragon* behind while I swam. If I had to dive down and look at something, I would let the rope go and retrieve it afterwards. I put on the fins and mask and eased into the water.

The crackle of the living reef and the cacophony of its dwellers at work always encouraged me when I first got overboard on diving trips; there was a big catch waiting for me somewhere on this reef today. I jumped from the dry into the underwater village hard at work below, hustling just like me. The crunching of parrot fish as they bit into something on the coral was followed immediately by a trail of excrement. I could hear the chatter of grunts as they flowed in urgent schools in between the elkhorns and sea fans. The booming bass of a grouper holed up in a shady rock warned an intruder who had strayed too close. I prayed silently, saying things like, "Almighty God, I'm not a greedy person. I don't want too many lobsters or fish, just enough to supply my humble kitchen and feed my small family... but there again, Heavenly Father, if you could see your way clear to providing me with that big catch then I would be eternally grateful." Of course these prayers were sincere at the time but on the occasions that I did have a good day and was knocking the rum back, I would forget to give Him thanks. Foxhole prayers they were called.

I dived for maybe an hour without seeing anything except the intact, recently-shed shell of a lobster lying down at the mouth of a hole. I felt the rush of hope taking the breath to go down and hook it, only to find it hollow. I was also fooled repeatedly this day by dead sea fans whose branches protruded from rocks and crevices mimicking lobster whips. Around 10:00, with nothing to show for nearly four hours of diving against a strong current, I decided to get in and smoke the second cigarette and paddle down to a series of patch reefs to the north of where I had been.

At one of these patches, a big tiger shark had chased Dave-O and me onto the shallows and had swum around as if waiting for us until Dave-O frightened it away by diving down and swimming up at the monster, yelling through his bubbles while blasting from his snorkel. The patch is identified by an anvil-shaped rock sticking out of the water. At times a pelican sits on this anvil rock. An older head in Helene told me once that when a pelican sits on the rock, there are lobsters in some of the special holes. On this day, there was no pelican sitting on the anvil, but I decided to try anyway. The older head was not wrong. I scoured the patch on the sides, on top, and underneath the staghorns, but there was not even a sign of anything edible. Under one of the ledges off the edge of the patch at about five fathoms, I thought I saw the telltale pieces of freshly-cracked shell that indicated lobster were living there. I took the breaths and dived down, being careful to keep a man's length distance between me and the cave so as not to startle the bugs and run them back in. Once at the bottom, balancing myself on fingertips with my neutrally buoyant body, I peered inside and was rushed by a huge green moray with its beady, zombie-like eyes and gaping mouth with that one long fang hanging from its top jaw. I got to the surface choking since I had taken a breath of saltwater in my moment of panic. Looking back down, I saw that the moray had decided to abandon its cave and was slithering back down into deeper water.

At around 1:00, I headed toward Pascual Bight. Edward Palmer, known as Tiger, who was the caretaker at Pelican Point on Barbarat, was sitting on the steps of his shack and as I passed close by, he yelled something to me as was his custom. I barely made out the words "Limey" and "salt lucked." This was not uncommon, as he barely had a conversation with anyone without doing so in the most derogatory terms. I just waved my paddle in the air and smiled, although I didn't feel like it, and kept on going my way. I think he was this way because he had worked for many years when he was younger as a ship's bosun. Tiger was also quite a songwriter in his own right, penning such local calypso classics (albeit in his head) as "Brown-Skinned Girl, Stay Home and Mind Baby" and "Three Risings on My Nutsack." He would sing, Martin Forbes would keep the beat with the spoons, Uncle John Martinez would play the saw, and Truman was on the coconut grater. Of course, Heslow would keep the rhythm with his six-string. Tiger was making a signal with his arms pointing towards the west.

At about this time, I noticed that after the flat calm day there was a slight wind beginning to pick up from the west, which meant that I would have a battle on my hands steering *The Dragon* back down to leeward into the jaws of a west wind. The norther was obviously moving in on us faster than expected. With all my preoccupation with not catching anything, I had failed to notice the change in the weather. The prospect of the difficult trip back, being tired and hungry and with nothing to show for my efforts, made me all the more despondent, but I still had an inkling that I was to hit luck and so I got overboard at the reef at Pascual Bight. I had to dive deep here because the holes were in some muddy ledges at the foot of the reef, at the point where it slopes down into the muddy seabed, beyond which tanks were needed. I had heard some of the more seasoned divers saying that there were huge trees of black coral down past this point. In shallow water you could afford to dive down and inspect each rock; however, diving deep areas you had to conserve energy and couldn't just keep diving down deep to check every rock and ledge. You had to look for signs. Small scraps of white shell at the mouth of a rock hole or ledge or evidence of "brushing" of the lobster whips on the sandy seabed were proof that a lobster had recently lived or was living there. Needless to say, there was little or no evidence that any lobsters had lived anywhere on this reef recently. I didn't even see a fish or a conch. After each deep dive down, when I came to the surface my head felt lighter and the hunger started to bite.

On diving days, I was always ready to head back down around 2:00, and on a normal day I would have had at least a pound of lobster tail, a conch or two, and a smattering of fish. I resolved to keep trying in that stubborn way that I most disliked about myself. I sacrificed my fourth cigarette, and while I paddled to my last resort reef, which was located close to shore on the westernmost tip of Barbarat, I noticed with some concern that the west wind had not died down by any means. In fact, it had strengthened and there were some hefty white horses galloping along out behind the reef about two hundred yards from shore. I dived for the best part of an hour-and-a-half with no results; the only brief respite was when a fairly large mackerel passed below me at a leisurely pace. Despite my efforts, I was too slow getting the speargun out of the dory and the water was too murky. I lost him and was left with only the adrenaline coursing through my veins.

At 4:00, I decided that it was time to pack it in, and with nothing caught in the dory, no more cigarettes, and the prospect of forcing The Dragon through a truculent west wind, I started the lonely voyage back east to the island village where I lived. *The Dragon* was in its usual form, particularly as I passed the bogue between Morat and Barbarat and a strong current from north to south began pushing me farther away from land. The wind keeping me back had to be about twenty knots; it was two lengths forward and one back. Night began to fall before 6:00, at which point I was off Co-Co Plum Cay and outside the reef. I should have been inside it already, pushing *The Dragon* along the shallow bar. My strength was failing me by this time, and I was spitting chalk and feeling cramps in my stomach. I resolved to paddle perpendicular to the reef and try to reach the bar and push myself along it. At least I would be safe in shallow water and the reef would keep me from drifting to the mainland (as I had played it out in my panicking mind's eye).

It was close to 7:00 when I began to push myself along the last hundred yards of sand bar on the last stretch home and heard several motor dories with their distinctive lawnmower sound headed east to where I had come from. I could make out several men in each dory shining flashlights in every direction. They must have been looking for bait; sardines, I reasoned. By then I was exhausted and intent on reaching home and getting food.

It was around 8:00 (I tell you "around" or "close to" because I didn't wear a watch in those days) when I closed in on the family wharf. It was pitch dark so they couldn't have seen me. I could smell fish frying in coconut oil on a wood stove and my senses, alerted by hunger, could even pick out that it was *Craboo* wood burning. I could see a few people through the window of the bush kitchen by lamplight. I made out the stern face of my mother-in-law who had her arms folded in front of her and seemed to be presiding over the mourning that was apparently taking place. She had a demeanour that could only be construed as indifference tinged with disdain, as if to say, "come on now, they aren't worth all that much fuss!" Who on earth could have died? No one in the yard was infirm. What struck me as strange was the sound of sobbing from various women, but one particular voice that was familiar to me was my wife's. She was talking while sobbing intermittently with such sincerity that it resonated a deep sorrow within me. "I shouldn't have let him go out on an empty stomach. I should have been happy to get up and get him his breakfast. He told me that something would happen to him and now it has."

Closer to me, two men stood up with their backs to me looking on at the "mourners," which is why they hadn't noticed me easing in on my last legs (or shoulders). They discussed the route that various motor dories in the search party for me had taken and should take in order to find me, my body, or signs of me, given the currents and wind directions. One of the men was old man Willis, my father-in-law; the other man was another son-in-law of his, also a free diver. Their attitude was grave yet pragmatic, as if this were not the first mishap they had witnessed at the hands of Mother Ocean. It was an uncanny experience and was as I had always imagined death, with the deceased looking over the mourners and loved ones and being able to hear everything they said.

When we are gone from this world, I have often wondered since that day: on our way to meet our maker, will we be afforded the selfish privilege of looking back over those who mourn us and those who don't?

I was filled with remorse at having behaved so selfishly in the morning with my wife and resolved that evening after the hugging and relieved laughing and joshing to take a trip down to Oakridge the next day and seek steadier employment.

Old Dogwood Post

It was around 5:00 in the evening, not that many noticed, and a group of Black men of varying shades were gathered casually to form a circle around a stump that rose three feet out of the ground. Some of them sat on an upturned dory that was having a new keel fitted, the fresh shavings of which lay in golden curls in the dirt of the seashore below their feet. Some men smoked to run off the sandflies that now rose from the ground in invisible platoons to torment them, as they usually did at this hour when the breeze was scarce. Others swiped at them with towels or tablecloths, and a few slapped their ankles and necks, sucking short gasps of air between clenched teeth as they grabbed at the stings of the ones they were too slow to kill.

Most of the group had finished their work for the day and were washed up and changed. Most wore T-shirts and vests with shorts or jeans. Some wore flip-flops that they called "rock-n-roll slippers," and the rest were barefoot. All had worked hard in the sun since before dawn—some diving, some fishing, one woodworking, two cutting house posts. They each felt a contentment as one does after a hard day's sweat and a good wash afterwards. They also felt a kinship to one another, not because they were in some distant way or another related but because they were humble island folk who had battled another day against adverse conditions as they and their proud people had done for

150 years since the emancipation to eke out a meager existence from the sea and the land. Each man in his own way had done or seen something special that day that had made it particularly unique. Dave-o had seen a huge turtle on long reef in shallow water that he was not able to catch. Eddie had observed a shark fighting an alligator while he was out fishing deep water. James had discovered a beehive that he would smoke tomorrow to steal its honey. Sam had caught a large queenfish,* the first of the season, that weighed in at over forty pounds. Each had mentioned to the rest, unprompted, about the day's events. They did not interrupt one another, maybe owing to the mutual respect with which they held each other, but more so to the interest that they all shared in nature, the land, and always that which would forever surround them: the sea.

Despite the flies, the men were comfortable. It was their favourite time of day. There was no noise, save for the slap and rustle of palm branches waving in the gentle blow from the east, the near distant chanting of children in the bight as they skipped barefoot over a piece of black rope. In the harbour near where they sat, a boat engine thumped a steady baritone as it pumped its bilge. From a nearby bush kitchen wafted the simple doughy smell of flitters and coconut oil as a woman prepared someone's supper under lamplight on a mud stove that always made the food taste better, they often agreed.

One of the men, the oldest in the group, whose real name was Olna Forbes but was known to all as Uncle Bubu (no one could remember the origin of the nickname) was not washed. In fact, he seldom washed, for no one had seen him do so and the years of grime etched into the brown folds on his neck vouched for this widely held assumption. He had just come from his plantation in the flat land and had a sack full of coconuts and roots. He had set his sack down and lodged his machete with a deftness of his wiry forearm into the stump (which was actually an old house post)

14

around which they all gathered. The house post, Bubu had told them on many occasions (lest they forget), had been there for over a hundred years and once formed part of the the house of the late Baptist Bowman, freed slave and founding patriarch of the small island. The post was cut from the Iron Dogwood tree, the strongest and longest-lasting of all posts. The fact that it had weathered a hundred years of storm, rain, high tide, and machetes was a testament to its usefulness.

Bubu drew up an old soda crate washed ashore in last September's high tide, pulled a blackened, crudely rolled cigar from the breast pocket of his sweat-soaked, bush-stained shirt, and bit off a thumb-sized plug which he lodged in his hairy maw between tooth and cheek. He grinned after he did this, for he knew that all eyes were upon him as he performed this strange-to-many bygone habit that set him apart from the rest. This was a signal to him that he had everybody's attention, in which he reveled, so that he could begin talking. Many of the old man's stories were heavily embellished, but because it was fun for the younger men to coax these crackers from him as a barracuda takes to a sprat tow-bait, they normally grinned—some choked on their laughter—during his fragments from the past. Bubu with his tall stories was just as much part of this island's tapestry as the drab green oak trees covering the hills that loomed over the group and behind which the sun set as he began yet another tale.

"I hear you all talking about big queenfish, and that's true, we get 'em big here and on the banks, but on the ocean in deep water, none of you have seen anything like it."

He hawked a large wad of tobacco juice to the ground and took a large suck from a half-bottle of cane spirit that someone had left carelessly on the carpenter's trestle table to his left.

"They say that the American record for the queenfish is 130 pounds, which is a good size and I don't doubt... but they grow bigger 'round Cuba... Cape San Antonio... actually I've seen the biggest kind right there. It's owing to the fact that Castro hides that kind of thing up there that the Yankee doesn't know about. The fishing banks of Cuba are some of the richest in the world."

He grinned at this, showing yellow ivory that had not seen a toothbrush in decades but was kept strong by the sticks of cane that he sucked in the bush during the day to keep his appetite down.

"I was working on the old *Marjorie E.* running bananas and coconuts to Tampa in those days with poor old Captain Lem, around about the same time I had just got married to my first wife, God rest her soul. We always used to put out a line, 300-pound test, once we left Roatan offa the West End point. We used a special Norwegian hook on it and something tough like a Barra' belly for a tow-bait. Only this particular trip that I'm talking about, the cook—some fella out of Punta Gorda—forgot to get the bait and so I decided to try out my luck with a piece of red handkerchief that I found in the lazarette by tying it to the eye of the hook. I fixed it up good style and pelted it overboard, the whole crew killing themselves laughing. That was midday, the whole of that night, and the next day—nothing. I was sure the damn piece of red cloth was salt. By this time on the trip before that we had the ice-chest full!"

The smell of kerosene now permeated to where they sat as lanterns were being lit and etna stoves primed in nearby houses for the night.

"I was bosun's mate in them days, and I had just finished my shift and decided to smoke a cigarette on the back deck before dinner. I went down and sat on a coil of rope looking out at the wide-open ocean, catching a glimpse on the far horizon of Cape San Antonio, Cuba."

Without many of the group noticing, a small elderly man whom people called Black Cat had shuffled in to join them, ostensibly to bum a cigarette from somebody. Now he had his smoke and he sat listening.

"I checked the lines," continued Bubu, "but they still lay the same. One mind told me to pull it up to check the bait. I finished my smoke and started to haul up the heavy line. It was damn heavy, mind, 'cause the boat was doing eight knots in that heavy surge off the island of Cuba. When I had her halfway up, I felt a jerk and before I knew what had happened, ten fathoms of line were back overboard and smoking over the watertop. I tell you, the line went so tight you could play fiddle on it! All I could do was send tell the mate to slow her down and holler for my shipmates to help me pull in the line and whatever it was on the end.

"It took six of us two hours to pull that son-of-a-gun in. All the while we thought it was a bull shark owing to its pull and how it kept bucking from one side to the next. When the end of the line was about eight fathoms from the boat stern, the fish made one leap into the air (must have jumped all of twelve feet high) so that we could see his white belly and silver sides with blue tiger stripes, knowing then that he was a queenfish. And what a one. Only one time, when he was close and he could feel the wash of the big propellors and the noise of the boat, did the beautiful animal try to dive for bottom. We made a wrap with the line around a cleat, and he came to the top, his eyes as wide open and black as pot bottom. His mouth kept opening and closing like he was gasping for breath, and he chewed on the piece of red cloth like he wanted to finish eating it before we got him on board."

Although the assembled village men each had different callings, all were fishermen at one time or another and knew the sea, its creatures, and its moods, as one does a special place that can be remembered over and over again with fondness since the beginning of memory. These island men, as do all of the same ilk, loved a fishing story. All were held in trance, relating to every flourish of Bubu's word picture.

"When we had him 'longside the vessel we had to use a cathead on an outrigger to haul him up. We couldn't do it between us, so we used the winch. Thank the master he was hooked good!"

"How much pounds did it have, Uncle Bubu?" One of the younger men asked the question for everybody, the hint of a grin at the corners of his mouth.

"Well, my friend, you mightn't believe me, but owing to the fact that we didn't have a big enough scale on board there was no way to tell. But I do know one thing, though—it took us 'til 7:00 that night to link him up and when we had done—not counting the head and the tail—all the links filled up a fifty-five-gallon drum. It had to have been well over 350 pounds!"

"Raas!" said one man.

"Bitch!" said another.

"Boy, he could lie!" muttered a small voice.

Suddenly, someone let out a mocking bellow of a laugh, much larger than belied his small frame. It was Black Cat.

His real name was Davis and he was nearly as old as Bubu, if not older. He was a bit of a loner and he only talked to most people when he was drunk. Most of the time he greeted people with a quirky "How, How!" that made people chuckle in much the same way that Bubu did with his tobacco chewing. Not much was known about him, only that he had left the island as a young man and returned in his fifties after travelling the oceans as a merchant sailor. It was said that he went ashore in Brazil long ago, got drunk, lost all his documents, was left behind by his ship, and stayed there for a long time catching rare butterflies for collectors to make a living until he had enough for his passage back home.

He was small but had wide shoulders and the big forearms common to men who have worked boat decks for any length of time. The craggy skin on his charcoal black face seemed to tell the wretched tale of Davis's lonely life at sea, gazing at endless horizons on nameless oceans day after day, interspersed only by bouts of whoring, heavy drinking, and barroom brawling. Now in his other, older life he lived a painfully harsh existence working a small plot of inherited land with his hands, now gnarled and twisted with arthritis, growing plantains, watermelon, and wongler seed, which he dried and used to make candies for the children. Davis was noticed most by people, however, for his beautiful straight hair that was snow white and soft as cotton and that gathered in babyish curls at his shirt collar to give him a rather rakish appearance. People said that he had hair like that because his great-grandmother was a white woman from England.

Because he always looked so serious and only spoke to others when he was drunk, it was a rare treat to hear this enigmatic old hermit give an opinion about something other than the weather. He even surprised himself when he opened his toothless mouth to speak.

"Well, Olna, I'll tell you and the rest something else. I was working on a freighter run across the Pacific from the Panama Canal to Hong Kong, China as a quartermaster's mate. I used to put out a line also, although the fish in those oceans are different to ours we have 'round here, but they taste about the same to me. I suppose it's fish wherever the hell it is!"

This brought a ripple of chuckles from the assembled, and Bubu, a little peeved at having the limelight stolen away from him, began rustling through his digging sack as if preparing to leave. Noticing that the men were paying attention to what Black Cat was saying and sensing an unsettling purpose in the little white-haired man's voice, Olna folded his arms defensively and listened to the rest.

"We also had a line out from the back deck," Black Cat continued in his hoarse drawl. "It was a thick line and... anyway, it looked damned strong. We had it out for a couple of days also.

Nothing." He seemed to pause after every thought. Chomping at his gums, nose tilted slightly toward the night sky searching, it seemed, for the direction in which he should head with the tale. "On the third day we were off the island of something or another—it was so small it was a cay, really—when the line went tight." He paused again but this time for effect that was hinted at in the rumour of a smirk that seemed to provoke little dimples to appear in his cheeks below the eyes. "And do you know what it was?"

No one answered. They merely grinned, surprised by the welcome presence of Davis with a story, albeit brief, from his adventurous, secret past.

"It was a large ship's lantern," said Black Cat without cracking a smile, "and it was still lit!"

With that he took a large swig from the open bottle that stood on the carpenter's trestle and looked steely-eyed at everybody in the group until his eyes met Olna's.

"How in the hell do you expect us to believe that yarn?" said Olna with a sheepish half-grin, not knowing what to make of the group's ominous silence and the disquieting briefness of the tale.

"Well, Bubu, I'll tell you what," said Davis, breaking out now into a broad grin that exposed well-worn gums that had been doing his teeth's job for years. "If you take 150 pounds off your fish, I will turn off the ship's lantern."

With this he smoothed his beautiful white hair down on his skull with one hand, the other in his pocket, and basked for a moment in the thick, racking laughter that his tale had brought forth from the men before he turned and with small, steady steps made his way into the darkness, back to his house for supper.

The men were still laughing and slapping their thighs and each other's shoulders as Bubu spat out the tobacco, mounted his sack on his back, and pulled the machete from the post with a squeak of its blade, exposing a sliver of yellow dogwood the same colour it had been when first cut from the forest so long ago to build the house in the same spot they gathered that night to talk and listen.

German Man

I had heard of the man before I met him in person. He was known to the villagers as "German man." His reputation preceded him, and after hearing stories of his antics, I visualized him as a mountain of a human being. In reality, he was short, his back humped by age and his blond hair long and straggly—God alone knew when it had last been washed. Being a commercial diver and underwater welder by trade, he had been taught freediving by the men of Helene just as I had, and he was pretty good at it apparently. The favourite story as told by the Helenians of the German man was the fact that often he would swim out past the reef to dive with nothing but basic diving equipment—mask, snorkel, flippers—but towing behind him a steel washtub in which he kept his hookstick and speargun. One day he shot a mutton snapper in Rocky Point Channel and the tiger shark that lived in the vicinity (it had taken several snappers from me in the past also) rushed in to take it from him, but he would have none of it and kicked the shark on his nose while holding the speared fish behind him and then lifting it into his washtub. The shark, incensed by the blood in the water and enraged that it had been cheated of the morsel, chased after the German man for half a kilometer to Bentley Bay, all the way to the beach in front of his house while he fought off the constantly circling and rushing beast. "German man hard, boy," the Helene men used to say, and he gloated over this reputation, for a while.

His real name was Adolf Ulrich, and he indeed was German. The first time I met him, he was drunk and unimpressive. He was buying some kerosene at Leonela's store, which was next to where I was living then. We had never been introduced but he obviously knew by hearsay who I was. It wasn't difficult since there were only three white men living on a three-mile by one-mile island with a population of 450. He took a wide stance, as many drunks do, swaying from north to south and looking at the front of my house, mumbling something unintelligible that sounded friendly. I thought I heard "fucking ath hole." He had a lisp that was more pronounced as he became drunker. When I related this to my first friend I ever had in Helene, Baldhead, he laughed and suggested I not take him seriously since everyone knew that he was an obnoxious drunk. He was tolerated and teased as well but respected as an experienced and brave diver.

The next time I met him, he was sober. I was in search of guavas on my day off from teaching English at the village school and Baldhead knew where there was a guava patch behind Bentley Bay. As we came out of the bush, our bags full of guavas, we came upon his small wooden house where he had just come in from the sea and was lying in his hammock watching his wife Vida (known as *Cousin Vida* and pronounced "wider") chipping coconuts to put them to dry as copra, which is what she was known for. I could see he had come in from diving since there were three large fresh lobster backs on the shallow seabed through the clear water next to his small wharf. Smiling, Cousin Vida called us over since she was, in fact, Baldhead's cousin; the entire population was related. She must have been in her fifties and had a lovely smooth skin and perpetual smile. She oozed kindness and humility.

"I'm so happy to meet you and so thankful for what you are doing for our youth here on Helene. He is my husband, Ulrich." She motioned to the German man in his hammock.

He didn't smile; later I realized he rarely smiled unless drunk and being sarcastic or provocative.

"Yeah, man, nice to meet you." It was as if he had no recollection of that day in front of my house or maybe he was too embarrassed to acknowledge that we had met before under such circumstances. He had a thick, slurred speech, notably Germanic but using American slang which gave me the impression that he had lived around Americans for some time. I was not mistaken. He had actually been born in Breslau when it was Germany (it is now the Polish city of Wroclaw) and as a teenager emigrated to the United States, following his older brother to California. A quick way of gaining legal status was serving in the armed forces and Ulrich signed up and served five years in the 82nd Airborne, as a baker no less. In one of those quirks of coincidence, years later this was confirmed to me by a fellow paratrooper of his who also happened to live in the Islands.

By now he and I were in deep conversation, more like an interrogation on both ends, him in his hammock, me sitting on an upturned bucket. Baldhead and Cousin Vida were sitting on the rickety wooden steps to the house, carrying on their own conversation, gossip punctuated by bursts of raucous, leg-slapping laughter. He was a different person from the drunk German man I had met previously, not a studied man by any means, yet wise. He was engaging, perhaps because he didn't much get the opportunity to have a decent conversation. After his service in the Army, he took up apprenticeship as a welder and later branched off into marine welding which is what brought him to Helene. He'd worked on the treasure salvage vessel, *The Rambler,* that had sunk during Hurricane Fifi in 1974 and whose wreck could still be found in the shallows of Port Royal, two kilometers west of

Helene, as a home to hundreds of red grunt. Actually, *The Rambler* had made quite an amazing discovery of what was a wreck of indistinct origin loaded with amphoras that, when dated using a special method at the University of Pennsylvania, were found to be made in 1200 AD, over three hundred years before Columbus was supposed to have discovered the Americas. Ulrich said an archeologist on *The Rambler* suggested that the Chinese may have been trading in these waters before the so-called discovery of the Americas. Strangely, the permit was cancelled by the Honduran government soon after the amphora discovery, and the project was forgotten and shelved.

The German man stayed, however. He was simple, not given to much luxury, and he enjoyed the Helene lifestyle of fishing, diving, subsistence farming, and rum drinking and carousing at the weekends. He found out that he could go to work plying his trade as a welder and boilermaker in America or Germany, living frugally for four or five months at a time, then come back and live the rest of the year in the relative comfort to which he had grown accustomed. He met Vida, who had two sons already, at a dance. They shacked up and he finished raising her boys, Eddie and Billo. There was no electricity, just kerosene lanterns. His only creature comfort, like mine, was a small leather-bound shortwave transistor radio on which he listened to Deutsche Welle, Voice of America, and the BBC. Actually, this radio was the subject of a German man story amongst the Helenians. When Germany lost to Argentina in the World Cup final of 1986, enraged he stood up at the final whistle and smashed the radio to the floor; later, drunk, he had been seen crying over it wanting to listen to the news. I enjoyed my visits to his simple yet cozy board house on the beach and his whimsically gruff Teutonic style of conversation; I visited at least once a week. I asked to go diving with him on one occasion, although everyone said that he dived alone, and he scoffed. I was still learning then but was developing the skill and beginning to feel comfortable in the saltwater on the reef.

"You think you hard already, man? You think you can keep up with me, man? You not ready yet. Maybe one day in a few years' time—hah!"

I humoured his lighthearted scorn, which frankly I found mildly intimidating, but he was my elder and a diver of much experience whom I held in high esteem, mainly because he had earned the respect as a competent and brave free diver from the Helene men. He left soon after this exchange for California, this time to work on a contract at the shipyards in Long Beach.

He was gone for months and during this time I had stopped teaching for a month or two and dived every second day, leaving the house at 4:00 a.m. and paddling the long distances to the best reefs, channels, and patches. I didn't have the experience or technique that the Helene men had, and I begged to be taken with them which was enormously generous of them since it was an unwritten code that whatever a pair of divers caught, the proceeds were to be split evenly. The first few times I went diving with a partner I would probably hook at three or four lobsters and be lucky to catch one, while my partners would catch seven or eight but would still share the money down the middle. They were always patient with me, as I am sure they were with Ulrich in his day and with all of the youth who were learning this trade.

During this learning process I had hooked at lobsters on a few occasions and missed them and broken off whips or toes. In most cases the "bug" would tuck itself deep in a rock where no one could get it and we would lose money, but there was never a harsh word. The toughest rebuke I faced was a singsong sigh from a tired partner. "Oh Lord, Matt, doon worra, we'll soon get couple." It reminded me of how it was learning to bat in cricket as a youngster when I would lose my wicket early without scoring a run and the coach would say in that patient voice that wasn't at all patronizing but full of hope that one day I would get better, "Not to worry, Harper, it's all on the up and up from here!"

I had always expected my biggest challenge to be getting in and out of the dory without rolling it over but it ended up being easier than anticipated. I wouldn't consider myself clumsy, but I found activities that involved balance quite challenging. This activity involved lots of upper body strength which, thankfully, I had. The dory itself was a little wider than hip-width and so the secret to getting in from the water was to grasp each side with both hands and lift the upper body out of the water with the arms and shoulders whilst kicking with the flippers. Once parallel with the thwart, one would swing their backside in. Getting out into the water was exactly the opposite procedure, making sure to hold the sides of the dory so as not to flip it, although it was difficult to flip because most paddling dories were akin to upturned bananas. But it did happen from time to time and for that there was a process of "unsinking" it, which involved pushing and pulling the dory lengthways in the water. This motion made most of the water rush out and the little that remained could be bailed out with a half-Calabash shell. Roley showed me these dory skills with much patience before he was knocked down and killed crossing a road in Santo Domingo with his Walkman earphones on which drowned out the sound of the oncoming truck. I became so proficient that within a few months that I was able to stand up in the dory and paddle which helped me get a better view of the surrounding reefs. I had mastered these skills at twenty-two years of age, whereas the Helene men were experts in it from toddlerhood. I always remembered Roley for this.

My skills both handling the dory and freediving did improve, such was my determination to be like these men and to to pull my weight and match the German man for the respect he held among them. The advantage I had was that I seemed to have big, strong lungs and powerful legs, probably from all the cross-country running and strength training I had done playing rugby at the highest level, and I developed into a deep diver with a seemingly natural ability to hold my breath longer than most, controlling my lungs to eke out the oxygen at the bottom. I was often challenged to dive for conchs on the north side of Barbarat Island and in the Morat Bogue where the conchs were eight or nine fathoms deep, with a current that made it like diving into a bowl of porridge. I became so competent at this that I was able to dive down, pick up a broad-leafed conch, swim to another along the seagrass bed, and then swim up with just my legs and flippers since my hands were occupied holding the conchs. I remember bringing up three on one occasion and, despite the fact I had my arms around the conchs as if I were rocking a baby, I broke the surface nearly down to my navel above the water top!

I realized that I was gaining respect and trust when I would complete a successful dive or bring up conch or lobster and my partner would look at me, grin, and give me that nod that said it all. When I dived with a partner we would spend around five or six hours in the water, swimming around shallow reef patches or looking down at deeper coral heads, looking for the telltale whip moving around in front of a rock fending off a fish. The whips looked like cockroach antennae from the water top and that would be when we would start the deep breaths—hyperventilation—and, on the third deep breath with the lungs fully expanded, bend at the hips and let our upper body weight and slow, steady fin kicking take us to the bottom where, if we were good, we would hook what we were after.

But the day came when I knew in myself that I had become a competent "frogman," as Uncle James Bodden would say. I was diving with Dave-O and we were off Long Reef in some beautiful white water about eight fathoms deep when I glimpsed a large, well-camouflaged hogfish leaning next to a sea fan, resting. It was about six feet from a pot loaf rock, also called brain coral. I pulled all three black rubber bands down onto the spear on my speargun, made sure the tip was screwed on tight so I wouldn't lose it, took my breaths, and dived down, clearing my head halfway as I always did by yawning with my mouth closed. By the time I had drifted close to the hogfish, he realized he had been spotted and flinched to make a dart for it, but I had him picked out and hit him in the sweet spot on the fleshy part of the back of his head two inches before his eyes. He trembled slightly and became still.

As I pulled the hogfish in with the spear string, I noticed a slight movement in the corner of my eye and turned to see two large white lobsters in a hole under the pot loaf rock, their long whips moving from side to side, seeking food, sensing danger. I left the speargun and dead hogfish on the sea floor and came up for air and my hookstick. By now Dave-O had grabbed the dory rope since I was towing it and had let it go to pursue the hogfish. I took my breaths and went down directly to the rock. The biggest lobster came out of the hole, lightly waving his whips at me, but I already had the hook under his chest plate in the sand and with a swift jerk of my arm paralyzed him with the hook and pulled him out croaking. No time to waste since I felt my lungs beginning to burn, I grabbed his back, drove the pointed end of the hookstick into his chest, and dropped him dead next to the hogfish. I went after the smaller lobster, which had gone a little further into the hole, and did the same thing except that I had no time to kill it and left it on the hookstick. By now I felt the urgency for air and swept up the fish, the gun, and the dead lobster, and pushed off from the sea floor, kicking upward. I could see the shadows of Dave-O and the dory eclipsing the sun at the surface and for as much as I knew I was getting closer to them, my lungs felt like they were bleeding and I wondered if I would make it at all. It seemed like an eternity to get there, and when I broke the surface I was seeing lights. Dave had already leapt into the dory and had a toothless grin on his face from ear to ear and just said, "Boy, you a hard man now... hardest white man in Helene."

"Harder than the German man?" I asked.

"Oh yeah, now yeah, way harder."

He had two smokes in his mouth; he lit one and gave me one, still grinning. It was if he were replaying in his head my antics down below at eight fathoms while he watched from above.

With growing confidence, I spent more time on the sea and the catches began to increase. I even began venturing off by myself if my regular partners were busy. I had begun to develop a knowledge of the sea, the reef, the quirks of the sea creatures, the movements of the tides, and the effect that the phases of the moon had on everything. My self-confidence was frightening and as I learned more and my skills improved to perfection, I became more daring and, I suppose, foolhardy to a certain degree. I had a distorted sense of my own invincibility, which I recognized viscerally as a danger. I absolutely immersed myself in the freediving life and culture, and everything I did was associated with it. I was by now making ends meet by doing it; by no means making a fortune but eating well three times a day and supporting my habits of beer, rum, and cigarettes. The diving equipment I was using I had brought with me when I arrived to teach, and thankfully I had purchased sturdy flippers, or *finfoot* as the Helene men called them, and a decent mask and snorkel. Little did I know that my decision to purchase robust equipment would serve me well later, diving most days for six or seven hours a day.

On Saturday nights we would gather at Myer's bar and have drinks. He had a Rock-Ola jukebox powered by a portable generator and for a "quarter" (50 centavos lempira) we could punch three songs. I only had one pair of shoes—Adidas running shoes—which I saved for special occasions and so most Saturday nights I walked the five minutes to his bar and did my dancing in my rubber flip-flops, or "rock-n-roll slippers."

I had heard it around the village that the German man had returned and frankly was looking forward to seeing him and reporting my progress, maybe even asking him to take me diving. One Saturday, soon after I had learned of his return, I walked down to Bentley Bay to see him, but Vida told me he was out diving. She made me some lemonade and we chatted a bit. That night I arrived at Myer's bar at 7:00 and he was already there—not too drunk yet but getting to the brink of being obnoxious. He had on a pair of jeans, some fancy black tassel loafers, and a white cotton button-up shirt which must have cost a penny. He was sporting a new Greek fisherman's cap from which his straggly shoulder-length blond hair emerged. He had put on some weight, which didn't suit him since we were always used to seeing his tough, sinewy frame bareback with no hint of a beer belly at all, even at his age. There was a half-empty liter bottle of Caña Brava rum on the table with an opened bottle of orange soda, and three of his Bentley Bay neighbours were sitting around the knee-high table on rickety wooden stools, tough divers and seamen all. I saw Sam Warren, his brother Juan Warren, and Richard "Park" Matute. Self-proclaimed "master of anything that creeps, crawls, or walks," Juan had an impressive Afro that was bleached all shades of yellow and red by the sun. He was the first to hail me in the weird silence between tunes on the Rock-Ola, which was punctuated only by crackling and hissing.

"Teacher, why have you stopped teaching our children to take up diving?"

"I'm challenging myself with something new, Juan. I'll be back teaching soon."

"You are a good teacher, young man, but these boys tell me you're a good diver now too."

I moved toward Ulrich to shake his hand in welcome, but his hostility towards me was tangible and I pulled my arm back and pretended to scratch my belly instead, ashamed of his slight.

At this the German grew irritated, glared at the four of us, and growled, "Give me my fucking bottle!"

He grabbed it and shuffled out of the bar uneasily down the dirt track to the dock where he had his dory tied up. It was an uncomfortable exchange, fueled by the fumes of white rum but more by jealousy, I could sense. Ulrich had enjoyed the reputation of singularly being the toughest white man or even foreigner to live the tough Helene life; maybe he perceived me to be a usurper. I told myself that it was the rum talking. All I wanted was his approval and acceptance as a diver, such was my adulation of this short, now slightly potbellied and humpbacked, troubled soul. I put it down to the rum and punched some tunes, smoked some cigarettes, and drank half an octavo of Caña V by myself at a table since the others seemed embarrassed by having sparked the German man's outburst.

I skipped diving for a couple of days to take care of my *ground* (plantation) where I had some cassava sticks planted that I was nursing into life. It was frustrating since the *weewee* ants would come in at night and eat all of the shoots that were trying to grow out. It was always disappointing to walk into the quarter-acre clearing of the forest, that I had cleared myself with axe and machete, to see the telltale trail of green leaf fragments leading back into the bush where the ants had marched in the previous night to chomp on my struggling cassava plants. It was small consolation that the banana and plantain suckers were doing well. I cleared away the weeds from around the crops and gathered some *cerasee* creeper to take back and boil. I gathered up a thick log of dogwood that I had been asked to bring for firewood for the mud stove. I missed the sea at that point and calm weather was coming up the next day—a Wednesday I remember well.

It was a good day for my partner Pandy and I. Glass calm sea, we made it to Yankee Joe Reef in one hour and, because it was calm, there was no current surge and most of the small crab holes in this shallow reef had a lobster in them. We moved to Long Reef and by 1:00 p.m. we had hit a deeper patch where we cleaned up and hit two good-sized mutton snappers with the gun. To top off a perfect day, the wind from the east began to pick up to a gentle breeze and we were able to drift down using a coconut limb for a sail while we ate sponge coconuts on the way back home. We would always say "going down" if we were travelling in a westerly direction with the east wind behind us, whether it was walking or paddling. The older heads would say "down to leeward" or, in the opposite direction, "up to windward."

We were back at the wharf by 3:00 p.m. and as usual everyone came out to see what was in the dory, the children running barebacked with their bare, dusty feet full of beach sand followed by a pair of scrawny but happy dogs, the grownups strolling in and swatting mosquitos with whatever they could get their hands on. The dory bow was red with lobsters—there were over fifteen, and it was close to seven pounds of tail in all. As Pandy was offloading our diving things onto the wharf and I was placing the lobsters to be headed then weighed, I caught a glimpse of a white man stepping awkwardly along the path toward us. It was the German man, shirtless, in a pair of cut-off jeans and his new Greek fisherman's hat. He was quite obviously drunk and the children, who were afraid of him anyway, began to run away. He added to their terror by growling and pretending to chase after them. Amid the shrieking of the fleeing children, he stumbled over to the entrance of the narrow wharf where we were now heading the lobsters and cleaning the snappers. He made a lunge as if he were to continue along the wharf and then with that horse sense that drunks possess decided against it. He stared not at Pandy but directly at me, with his arms folded in a whimsical way, almost a sort of dramatic posturing, swaying back and forth and fueled by the fumes of white rum.

"Pandy, you catch all of them stuff, man? Because you can't catch fuck, man." He was looking straight at me, his sardonic smile again goading me.

I didn't mind his insults, but Pandy was irritated. "Why don't you go back home to Cousin Vida, you old Gerry fool, before this Englishman puts his foot in your ass!" He looked at me and laughed in an attempt to diffuse the situation in case I was becoming annoyed. I wasn't though; my admiration for the German man was bigger than that.

He turned to leave and then stopped and looked back at us, issuing a challenge straight to me: "All these men talk about how tough you are and what a good diver you are now. You always want to dive with me—let's go tomorrow in my dory, on the Bank. Flat Rock must be full by now."

I knew what he was referring to. The Bank was a small seamount located a couple hundred yards offshore, but the best rocks were off the edge or in the deep between the island and the bank. However, the men mostly tanked it. It was dark and grungy down there, frequented by schools of blacktip sharks. I should have declined his challenge and accepted that he was still "the German man"—the toughest, foulest-mouthed, bravest, and still better than me. But I didn't. The need to prove my limits to myself and to attain respect in the village that was now my home were strong forces. I always called him Ulrich when speaking to him, out of respect. but today was different. I didn't feel it.

"Okay, German, tomorrow it is. Pick me up here at 7:00. I'll be waiting."

He glared at me for moment before he turned and left, more sure-footed than when he'd arrived, almost as if the exchange had sobered him up a bit.

Not really expecting him to show, I had an early breakfast of Cream of Wheat (my favourite before diving) which I prepared in the African way I had eaten as a child with melted butter, a sprinkle of sugar, and a ring of milk around it. I placed my fins, mask, and snorkel out on the wharf in an old flour sack in case he showed. At around half past 6:00 I heard his dory starting and then getting underway towards where I lived. His was one of only a handful of larger dories with engines, called motor dories on Helene, and each one was unique in the way it was painted or the type of engine it had. The German man's was the only one with a diesel engine, a two-cylinder, 800-rpm Lister to be exact, which was one of the most indestructible engines ever built. I walked out onto the wharf and saw him approaching, sitting on the engine box, slumped forward as usual and holding the steering ropes that were attached to the rudder. He was bareback and his stringy blond hair was, as usual, looking like it hadn't been combed, ever. He stopped the Lister a ways from the wharf and drifted in, grabbing at it when he was level.

"So, you ready, man? Or you want to chicken out? It's not too late." He was grinning that shit-eating grin.

"No, German," I said without smiling. "Let's go. We'll take Pandy with us to keep the dory up."

Pandy was mooching around the yard doing nothing. I bought us some smokes and he followed with a grin, anticipating some fun and perhaps some rum drinking after.

The Bank was close and so we got there quickly. I smoked on the way there, nervously I admit. The rock was found using an age-old method of lining up landmarks, in this case the wooden outhouse on Sam Warren's wharf in line with the shrimp boat wreck on Allen's Point to the west and then the southernmost tip of Ross Cay lined up with Tiger's house on Pelican Point on Barbarat. Once over the rock, which you can't see unless you are in the water, the German man and I put on our fins, rinsed out our masks, put them on, and slid into the water feet first over opposing sides of the dory. He indicated for me to go first, probably to see if there was anything there. After a minute I could see the faint

36

darkness of the rock below at around eight fathoms, large and flat like an enormous pancake. I took my breaths and flipped my ass into the air, the weight of my upper body taking me down, which was instinctive by now just like drinking water. I cleared my ears halfway down, but my head was tighter than usual. Maybe the night draught, I reasoned. It seemed darker than normal, and under one of the ledges I made out three lobsters, one large male and two females. I wasn't prepared to hook them so I started my way back up, making a sign by raising three of my fingers on my right hand to indicate three "bugs" in the rock. I expected the German man to offer to go down to give my lungs and head time to recover, but he yelled at me from ten feet away that he wasn't.

"You go down again. Let's see this hard young man in action," he scoffed.

Pandy was egging me on and giving me encouragement. "Don't kill 'em down der, enuh will waste ya breath. Hook 'em and just bring 'em on di hook."

I went down once more and felt my head tight again. I had to pause to clear my head, which wasted my air and made me lose momentum. Level with the ledge where the bugs were, I decided to go for the big, bleached male first, slipping my hook under his breast through the sand. I hooked up and out sharply, starting to feel my lungs burn. I grabbed his back and, letting my pride tell my lungs to hold fast, hooked at one of the other females and started my desperate kick for freedom at the surface. About two fathoms up, the big male in my hand made a desperate flip of his tail and broke loose, coming to land on top of the rock. I didn't take my eyes off him on my way up, but the German man had already seen this unfold. Wanting to avoid the injured creature getting back into the ledge again where it was certain to bury itself deep in the rock out of human reach while the danger passed, he was already on his way down as I broke the surface with a huge gasp. I watched him on his way down, his cut-off jeans billowing around his sinewy legs, his wild unkempt blond hair waving gently like a dervish in the blue-black depths. He paused halfway down just like I had, obviously having problems clearing as well. He looked up, almost contemplating coming up again but with his pride at stake, he forced himself down nevertheless. The big male was still slowly crawling along the top of the rock, gradually nearing its hole, so it was an easy hook for the German man, who then proceeded down to the ledge to hook the remaining female. He desperately looked up and came kicking frantically and clawing his way up to the surface, his eyes as big as saucers through his mask. He lost his grasp on the hookstick and it went torpedoing down to the sea floor with the lobster in tow. I did the same as he had and sent myself down to retrieve the hookstick with the impaled lobster.

At the top it was a mess inside the dory. The German man had struggled to climb in and had taken off his mask, bleeding from his nose and left ear, retching bile and cursing black and blue in a German and English mashup. I was already sitting on the dory cap relishing the soothing effect of my first smoke after the dives. They were Royals and so after a deep draw a good cough was on the cards. Pandy offered the German man a smoke.

"Fuck you, man, you fucking ath-hole."

"You want to go and spear some fish at Rocky Point now?" I asked him.

"Do I look like I want to go spear fish with you now? You damned foolish-ass man."

Pandy sagged his shoulders and jumped up quick, as most Creoles do when they laugh, animatedly whilst letting out a silent laugh, all teeth, shoulders, and head.

As far as lobsters go, it was a tie. As far as egos go, the German man came off worse. He didn't speak a word on the way back to our wharf, and Pandy had to handle his dory back to Bentley Bay for him while he remained prostrate, unable to stand. He even told

Pandy to give me the three lobsters, such was his dejection. He never did any serious diving after that, just venturing close to home for fish and conchs for the pot, but no more deep diving.

Riding the high seas of my youth, I went on to learn tank diving which was just starting to become an option with the Helene men as the promise of big lobster catches went deeper. I saw him every now and again, and he had grown humbler towards me and was never rude, never swore at me just like he didn't with the Helene men, no matter how drunk he was. It would have been arrogant of me to think it was subservience, but I enjoyed the simple fact that I had come out best, physically, over this man who was so revered in those parts.

Vida died suddenly in her sleep a few years later; it can't have been easy living with him. He left for Germany for about a year and upon his return shacked up with Juan Warren's widow; Juan had drowned in Guanaja. One of the quirky things he did whenever he came back home, not trusting banks, was to store his cash in a large five-pound Milex powdered milk can that he buried in the grass on his backland and marking the spot, like a pirate, using objects only he knew about. One night, while drinking, he ran out of money and went frantically searching for his Milex can, having forgotten the exact spot. He dug about five holes unsuccessfully until he furiously started blaming his stepsons, who didn't take kindly to the accusation, which led to fisticuffs. He suffered a stroke and the last time I saw him, ten years after our day on the Bank, he had filled out a bit and walked with a stick, but he was happy to see me, and we sat and reminisced fondly of the old days. I was living a different life then, with a steady job and on the road to a successful profession with my own family. It wasn't long after that day I learned of his passing in Helene where he was laid to rest, but every time I pass over the Bank or by *The Rambler* in my boat, I always remember him.

Gladiator

I had become so wrapped up in my new life with my first steady employment and had dived right into learning the trade that would become my career that I gave little thought to my recent past. In all honesty, even my young family had taken second place to my ambition. But a day came when I was reminded. Out on Oakridge Cay on a stinking hot and muggy Monday, I was reading the last of the meters for the day when I saw the decrepit wood-hulled fishing vessel *The Gladiator* being towed out of the channel like a lame horse. It had been stripped of its outriggers and parts of its wheelhouse, moss in a green shawl reaching up to the gunwales suggesting that she had sunk down at the dock and had been there for a while until someone had pumped her out to tow her away.

I sat on a mangrove root and watched as *Sister Sacha*, a steel-hulled shrimper painted blue with white trim in the colours of Mariscos Bahia packing house, towed her a mile offshore and set her alight. I watched until she started to sink and I could barely make out the last of her, the mainmast that I knew for a fact had a hole the size of a grapefruit in it about four feet from the point disappearing below the horizon with *Sister Sacha* on its way back. It was with some regret and a feeling of nostalgia that I saw the end of a piece of my past being put out of its misery in that way. My memory was jogged into recalling the trips out to sea on her, particularly the last one, an odyssey that taught me a wealth not only about the sea but about myself and humankind.

It was one of those visceral moments when a journey or event is planned and something happens that triggers doubt, almost as if your still, small voice is communicating behind the veil not to go forward. The last trip I made on *The Gladiator* was just such a trip. But by the grace of God was I there that day, at age twenty-seven, watching the sinking of the vessel. I should have only made it to twenty-three.

At the time of the trip, or should I call it a voyage, the boat's owner (also her captain) had no money and was getting the boat ready with a bank loan and credit from the packing plant's supply house. This wouldn't have been that bad if he had not been inebriated from the very moment he woke up at 10:00 a.m. to the moment he passed out at nightfall most days. It was the rum that was doing it, Flor de Caña's Extra Seco, or cane spirit as we called it in Africa. We were given hope each day at midday when he had a two- to three-hour window of lucidity during the gap between his hangover diminishing with his first drink (if he didn't throw it up) and his mood turning into invincibility and supreme intelligence. It would go gradually downhill from there.

After that first drink, he would stumble the hundred feet from his house to the wooden dock, bareback, in shorts and flip-flops, the yellow gold chain with the Spanish doubloon draped on his hairy chest glinting in the sun. He would reach the boat, clamber on board, light a smoke, cough until his face was beet red, and proceed to berate and curse each one of us as we busied ourselves with our individual chores. His name was Robert McNab, and he was a very capable all-around boat man, as one had to be to own and skipper a fishing vessel. An immaculate boat handler, superb mechanic, and one of the best navigators in the harbour, he had the fishing banks of Honduras, Jamaica, Nicaragua, and Colombia mapped in his mind. He had worked for McDermott as a Chief

Engineer for several years in the Middle East oil fields, where he had saved to buy his first boat. But he was going through a bad patch, as we all do when we let our bad habits dominate us. Having been on a drunk for two months, the boat tied to the dock all that time since the previous trip, the bank manager calling every week, his wife Elly was doing the best she could to keep her own house in order and maintain an appearance of normalcy to the creditors. The crew, myself included, had done well on the previous trip but the money was beginning to dwindle away for as much as we tried to stretch our lempiras, and we all feared we would soon be begging for credit at the stores again.

Those were trying times, with lots to do around the boat to prepare for the trip and no budget to speak of. Two of the three main compressors had to be overhauled; Harlan Webster, an outside help from Coxenhole, took care of this for Robert and Elly in exchange for meals, rum, and weed. He would carry his "tools," which consisted of a set of Allen keys, a crescent wrench, a hammer, a chisel, and two screwdrivers, around in an old croaker sack, his eyes as red as coals. The JABSCO pump needed replacing, the stuffing box needed repacking, the main engine exhaust flex needed brazing, the anchor chute needed welding, and the list went on. We suspected that some of the hull planking had popped loose, having not been on dock for caulking in over a year. Since there was no money to fix it, we had to to nail some tar-painted plywood sheets to the hull with Monel nails to hold them in like a soldier with a stomach wound holding in his guts with a battle dressing.

The crew were four of us besides Captain Robert, an interesting cross-section of the region and each one unique with his own idiosyncrasies. The Second Captain was Eduardo Calderon, known to us as Zarco for his striking green eyes, rare in a man of colour, and an impressive Afro. From Cauquira, he was a Miskito Indian, a former diver the Captain had taken under his wing and shown the trade. He knew the boat inside and out, from wheelhouse to engine room. Zarco had a twin brother who had been crippled by the bends after diving the spooky depths and heavy current of Misteriosa Bank in search of the giant lobsters that lived there; now relegated to a wheelchair and bed, Zarco paid for his care.

Johnny Cooper looked after the engine room and puffed out as much ganja smoke as the main engine when its injectors needed calibrating. Because of his shoulder-length hair, beard down to his chest, and youthful complexion, he looked like a Tretchikoff painting of one of the disciples or of Christ himself.

Abel was the compressorman, a pitch-black Garifuna from Iriona on the northern coast of Honduras, east of Truxillo, and the fact that he still operated three compressors was a miracle in itself. Five years previously he had been running a compressor on another vessel and had two tanks on the go, one of them having been there longer than needed. He hadn't bothered to check the PSI gauge. Having the munchies, he ducked into the galley for a bowl of rice and when he came back the tank exploded, throwing him against the winch and breaking most of the bones you could break in a human body as well as ripping open his mouth and leaving him with a terrible lisp and a pronounced limp. The scars on his legs were apparently terrible and he never wore shorts.

One-Eyed Dan was the cook from Bonacca and he was just that—one sharp eye always open and the other slammed shut forever. He never said much but would occasionally, and badly, break into an old Hank Williams Sr. tune.

Then there was me, assistant everything with barely a year of working on the banks but loads of enthusiasm, youth, and courage to make up for it. Primarily, I managed the scales at the end of each day, checking the conch or lobster that each diver brought in since the Captain trusted me implicitly. He also trusted me with the stores, groceries, cigarettes (which were checked out and charged to each diver and crew member), sundries like Andrews Salts that came in sachets and that the *Waiknas*—as we called the Miskito divers—would consume countless amounts of regardless of whether they had indigestion or not. More than anything Elly, Robert's long-suffering wife, trusted me with the money to buy the beef for the trip and the palm oil for cooking, both being much cheaper in La Mosquitia. I also carried the advance, 150 lempiras per diver, which was ostensibly for them to leave behind for their families to survive on while they were gone but in most cases were thrown away on *chicha* and beer before they left the beach.

The Captain and I had first met on Helene where I lived at the time since it was where my wife was from. Possessed with a youthful curiosity I had learned to dive, fish, plant, chop firewood, husk and chip coconuts, break and skin conchs, and all the quirky things an islander does. He was to complete my initiation in becoming an island man by taking me on the banks and teaching me about boats. He was up in Helene in his Boston Whaler on a drunk and searching for weed with his brother-in-law "Rabbit" and Johnny Cooper one weekend, and I participated in that drunk and ended up taking, plucking, and cooking one of my father-in-law's yard roosters at 1:00 a.m. since we were all hungry. I was being hospitable but the old man didn't see it like that, unfortunately.

He took a shine to me and was intrigued by my story, a public schoolboy from a good family who ended up in the middle of the Spanish Caribbean hustling to make ends meet. I often wondered about this myself but just knew in my heart that one day, somehow, it would pay off and I would be able to justify to my family the path I had chosen. Robert had also developed trust in me and frequently used me as a sounding board since I wasn't a "yes man" like Johnny or Zarco. Getting the boat ready for the next trip was dragging on and despite us working from dawn to dusk it seemed like we were taking two steps forward and one back. I was a handy welder with almost any metal, stainless, regular iron, or brazing flex pipe, and I knew how to calibrate auto-pilots and so I tended to busy myself with what was required.

Abel worked with Harlan on the compressors, Zarco and Johnny in the engine room changing filters and cleaning injectors and such. One-Eyed Dan was preparing the grocery list for the trip and cleaning out the day tanks, which were large rectangular tanks located on either side of the wheelhouse for storing the water used for drinking, cooking, and cleaning our teeth and washing our faces in the morning. There was not enough tank storage for all of us to even have bucket baths every day; it always ended up being once a week.

The Captain was more of a hindrance than anything else as the days wore on. During his windows of lucidity, he offered some advice and there was always a vague hint of his organization skills, albeit fleeting. We felt comforted to have him back since he knew more about boats and fishing than all of us put together. As the window grew shorter, he gradually became obnoxious and took his time belittling each of us one by one, and the tension began to build. Our patience would wear thin despite the high respect with which we held him, and we began answering him back and he would raise his gravelly voice and threaten to get out his pistol. That's when Elly would come out and take him home. Poor old boy, he was his own worst enemy and with the boat, his home, and property mortgaged it was all or nothing to keep the supply houses and banks from foreclosing.

We were all overextended. I owed the grocery a small bill that I couldn't pay, I had no savings, and would now have to go cap in hand and ask Mrs. Alice Bush for three weeks credit until I came in from the banks. My wife was two months away from giving birth to our first child, and I had to have the money saved to pay for the *granny* (the midwife) and to buy baby clothes and diapers and such, which I knew nothing about but was hoping my wife did. Johnny had a boy ready to start school and had to buy shoes and a uniform and books. Abel was building a small house in Iriona and owed the lumberyard. Zarco had a young family and his crippled brother to take care of. We were all feeling the desperation, but it was unspoken among us that once we got out to sea and the skipper sobered up and found his knack for finding conch and lobster, we would cash in and our woes would be a distant bad memory. The previous trip, two-and-a-half months prior, had ended in success with three hundred boxes and thirty thousand pounds of conch. The Captain had put us right on top of them on the 3 Nines Bank and then on Zapato Bank, so called because it resembled a shoe on the charts, and we hoped for the same fortune to repeat itself.

Once we were confident that the boat was somewhat ready to sail, we planned to leave on a Friday at 4:00 p.m. to steam through the night to be at Patuca by 7:00 the following morning, but ethereally we were being told not to. The day prior, a Thursday, we had gone to Gough's ice plant to load ice and groceries for the trip. As Zarco was bringing her astern, the D343 revving up, we were dead in the water, the main drive shaft going into overspeed and the prop at the bottom of the harbour. The large nut that held the prop in place had worked loose somehow and broken its weld. It was midday and we had no time—and Robert no money—to put her on drydock to refit the propellor. I knew about doing this in the water, having done it several times, and the water wasn't that deep where the prop had gone down. I just needed two fifty-five-gallon empty oil drums, a long chain, and two tanks. The method was to submerge the two drums, chain them to the propellor, and then with the other tank jetting air into the metal drum, displace the water. This would float the prop to the surface or, depending on how much air I let into the drum, float it to the level at which I needed to place it on the shaft. There were other steps I took to finish the task, including tightening the shaft nut by placing a pipe wrench on it with the handle directly under the hull while the engine was placed in gear full ahead which spun the shaft tightly onto the nut. This required some skill and deftness of hand, but Zarco did very well on his first time at it since the Captain was out of sorts as usual. It was exhausting work and took me four hours, at which point I was ready to get home and have my wife prepare some flitters and fried fish for me. We would still be able to sail the following day in the evening and I'd gained estimation from my shipmates.

My young wife, a traditional island lass from a God-fearing family as humble as they came, begged me not to go when I bid her farewell and gave her a hug with her seven-months belly and my pillowcase full of clothes (we hadn't a bag between us, let alone a suitcase), mostly cut-off jeans and T-shirts for a month. "Please don't go, Matt. God is tellin' enuh not ta go no weh... doh be so harden... please. What if something were to happen? I'm pregnant." With a lump in my throat seeing two tears rolling down her cheeks, I couldn't dare look back as I made my way in the skiff to *The Gladiator*.

The Loran was becoming at that time the indispensable navigational instrument, replacing traditional methods like the compass and the sextant, and that is what Zarco used to punch in the first waypoint, which was Cape Camaron or Camaron Point, 120 degrees east-southeast from Oakridge Harbour. The seas weren't bad as we left, maybe ten knots, enough to send Johnny down into the lazarette to go to sleep on a coil of rope as he usually did.

From Camaron Point we would steam coastwise to Barra Patuca where we would take on some supplies, beef, and *filipitos*, which were a type of rectangular banana that could be fried or boiled, plentiful on the Mosquito Coast. We would also take on around twenty divers and their dories as well as their dory men who would do the paddling and handling of equipment and product within the dory itself.

The Captain was in his bunk, passed out and hugging the rest of his half-gallon of Extra Seco. We all preferred he stay that way to sleep it off. If he woke up disoriented with the horrors of withdrawal, looking for a fight with one of us out at sea, it wouldn't end well. Zarco and I were in the wheelhouse watching the boat's bow drift up and down with each wave. It was a young moon so we could clearly see where the black sea met the sky with a wide sliver of moonlight making the night seem alive. A little after 8:00, Dan had a fish tea ready that he had made from a grouper's head and Zarco told me to take the wheel. Abel brought me my dish of soup which I picked at, not feeling particularly hungry, not that I would ever have admitted seasickness for fear of being ridiculed or called a *bean saver*. I had my tough man image to maintain, after all; as opposed to Johnny, who knew no shame. For me and others who would never admit it, the queasiness lasted for a day or two until we found our sea legs. I was steering with the auto-pilot which did everything, but I had to keep an eye on RPMs and speed to make sure we held her steady and on the compass to make sure we were holding the course, although the Loran would tell us this.

A little past midnight the wind started to pick up and I had to get out of the skipper's chair and stand up to disengage the auto-pilot and steer myself, grasping the spokes of the wheel. The ailing boat's timbers were creaking and complaining as we went up and down; the extended outriggers and their stays buckled and clanged each time the boat came out of a swell. Eventually I made out the lights at Camaron Point in the distance. They weren't city lights but the lights of hundreds of shrimp boats at anchor, probably heading off the catch that their nets brought in, in the first drag. All along this coastline was where the shrimp boats would drag their nets, which is why it was called Camaron Point because *camaron* is shrimp in Spanish. As we got closer, we could make out the crew on the well-lit back decks of the boats, barebacked and in shorts on little wooden benches heading the shrimp. I had also done that work before, heading the shrimp—separating the tail between forefinger and thumb and throwing the tails in the basket. *The Gladiator* was also a shrimp boat, but we didn't have nets or doors onboard; instead, our back deck was loaded with compressors and tanks and, in the next few days, loads of wooden dories. I hadn't heard Zarco walk up behind me until I heard him say in his halting English, "English, you go sleep now couple hours, next day we go Patuca, you the guy buy the cow and pay the advance."

I tossed and turned in my bunk but drifted off around 4:00 and at 6:00 was woken by the anchor being dropped. I got up to see the familiar sight of Barra Patuca, the mouth of the Patuca River that had its source five hundred kilometers away in Olancho. There was a sand bar there, hence the name. The village where we picked up the divers was situated on the banks of the river's mouth. The divers were all Miskito Indians with their own language that had many bastardized English words thrown into its vocabulary. Actually, the whole of the Moskitia Coast was a British colony at the same time as the Bay Islands; they used words like *espoon* (spoon) and *plateka* (plate). I had learned enough Miskito to get me into a tangle, but it was more convenient since I was learning Spanish at the time and most Miskitos had just the basic Spanish, much like the Bay Islanders. I had a little book where I wrote down new words as I learned them. It was with much satisfaction on a previous trip that I had announced to the divers' agent or *sacabuso*, "Pliscome boatwaya," or "Let's go to the boat now."

Just as soon as we were securely anchored, a half-dozen *pipantes* or "pitpans" as the islanders called them, were motoring out across the tan-coloured sea to greet us. The pitpans were hollowed-out tree trunks with a shaft and prop drilled out of the stern through a used flip-flop as a crude stuffing box so not too much water would get in. Attached to the shaft was any type of engine, the most popular being a one- or two-cylinder low RPM Lister which would make a lazy thudding sound and was why motorized pitpans were given the onomatopoeic name of TukTuk.

Everyone in them was standing up, in shorts, no shirts. The women were in short skirts or shorts and bras. One of them had on a T-shirt that read "Mondale Eats Quiche," probably from a clothing care package from missionaries. Whenever we arrived at Patuca, it always reminded me of the film *The Bounty*, when the vessel first arrived at Tahiti. Two of the pitpans were our divers coming to get diesel and any extra groceries they could scrounge— spaghetti, rice, flour. These were our two faithful divers, Nicodemus and Filiberto. They were not the biggest producers, but it didn't matter. If other boats came to look for divers in Patuca, they would wait for us, and this time was no exception. There was no electricity in Patuca except for one or two houses that could afford to purchase small, gasoline-driven portable generators at night. The diesel that they were looking to scrounge was for the *fifi* lamps, which were simple tin cans filled with fine river sand and a rope wick stuck down in the middle. The diesel was used to soak the sand, the wick was lit, and the house had a little light—enough to cook by and for the children to see to play with their little homemade stick figures. There were a few rough-looking ladies trying their luck. Most Miskito women had their front teeth missing for some strange reason, maybe because of the lack of dental hygiene and the prevalence of sugar in the diet.

After the initial excitement of our arrival had worn off and the pitpans had left with their pickings, Dan had us a breakfast feast of flitters, fried beans, and white cheese ready which we swiped down after the long queasy voyage over. Johnny claimed that he was so hungry he could "eat a horse and chase after the rider." I started to get my things ready because it was me who had the

51

money to pay the advance to the divers, buy a cow for beef for the trip, and get some *breadkind* for the meals. I normally spent a day and a night and came back the following day after completing my tasks, having slept wherever I could. There were no hotels or lodgings in Patuca, save for a Red Cross station that took in visitors but not commercial fishermen, unfortunately. I packed my books, ledgers, and a spare change of clothes—because I knew I was going to get wet getting to shore—inside a sturdy nylon bag used to pack the conch and tied it with netting twine. I was going to go with Abel and not Zarco who, although knowing the language and the people, had to stay with the boat until Robert came out of his funk and became the Captain again.

We pushed the boat's dory overboard, threw paddles inside it, and clambered down the side of *The Gladiator* to get into it. I tied my nylon bag to the painter so if we rolled over I wouldn't lose the money and the books. It got very rough close to the bar, and it would be a miracle if we didn't turn over. Abel, being the better doryman, was seated in the stern and I was seated on the thwart in the middle. The secret was to paddle with long, even strokes until you got to where the waves started to break and then to paddle fast to surf in on them until you hit the sand of the beach at the bar. We did so successfully on this occasion without turning the dory over. Once on the beach we pulled the dory up out of the high tide mark so she wouldn't drift away later. We walked to the village, barefoot just like the Miskitos, or *Waiknas*, which meant *man* in their language. However, they didn't really like to be called this, as it was too familiar.

Once in the village on the banks of the river, we found Nicodemus. A short man with a wisdom about him, always cheerful and smiling, he was in his mid-thirties but looked all of sixty. It was decided that I would stay with him during our time in the village, and Abel would stay with Filiberto. Word had spread that we were there, and a steady trickle of divers gathered around waiting for Matthias the *sacabuso* to begin the selection and payment of the advance. We only needed or could take twenty dories (a diver and his doryman who should also be able to dive in a pinch). Most of those selected had been with us for the previous trip, but there were several good producers whom we had lost to other boats in the long wait for us to get the boat ready. Matthias was not a diver; he just happened to be more educated than most *Waiknas*—I think he was an accountant—and charged a commission for what he did for us, which was to find the divers, negotiate the advance, and handle the final payment to each diver at the end of the trip.

It was simple. The diver would get perhaps two lempiras a pound for conch and six for lobster, and out of this he would have to pay his doryman, which was his own business. Many times, the diver would take a doryman who owed him money or perhaps a brother-in-law who stayed in his house in exchange for board and lodging. As crew we would be paid by the box (one hundred pounds). I was paid five lempiras a box whereas Zarco was paid ten as Second Man and Abel eight as compressorman. They were all lined up, chattering away in their singsong dialect which I found very quaint. I was always listening to try to identify the odd English word. It had taken me a while to realize that they called me *Mirikin* which meant "American,"; all light-skinned foreigners were referred to as such. The divers all lined up and since most were illiterate, Matthias had written their names in my simple ledger and they marked an "X" next to it and received their 150lempiras each as an advance. Being an isolated community, there was bound to be inbreeding and so half of the divers used the surname "Trapp." The other half were refugees from the civil war in Nicaragua next door which was reaching its end. They were from Bluefields and surrounding areas, mostly with English surnames like Coleman and Smith. Many of them would get drunk the night before sailing and their families would have to stretch what was left to buy basic grains and sugar. Of course, most of them raised chickens, pigs, and geese, and the children could hunt for iguanas, catch crabs, and fish in the river. Those who had cattle didn't need to go diving. It was 1988 and you got two lempiras to an American dollar.

By the time we had finished, it was mid-afternoon and Nicodemus's son had cut us ten bunches of *filipitos* and had them neatly stacked under the house floor, ready to be taken out on the river and onto the boat in his pitpan the following day. Filiberto and Abel were leading the cow they had chosen to the open lawn in front of Nicodemus's house and tethering it to a stake so it could graze. It was a scrawny-looking young bull, probably left to pick around among the riverside weeds for any grass. Times were tough for us as well as the owner, apparently, and the asking price was six hundred lempiras. It would be slaughtered and quartered tomorrow at dawn, ready to be taken aboard the next day. I paid the owner just as I had done with the divers, with scruffy notes that smelled of copper of ten, twenty, fifty, and one hundred that Elly had bound in stacks of five hundred with rubber bands that I had helped her to hide from Robert, lest he get hold of the stash and go on a road to nowhere. We had hidden the money in an empty fifty-pound butane tank that I had hollowed out the bottom of, placed the money in a brown paper bag inside, and tackwelded back together. Only the two of us knew about it sitting in the corner of their kitchen bodega.

After all was in order and prepared for the next day, I sat on the steps into Nicodemus's house and lit up a smoke. It was a pleasing scene at dusk, children playing with homemade spinning tops or *gigs* and the girls playing house among the tree roots with fowl clucking, crowing, and strutting around. Because it was a riverbank, the grass was lush and spongy and reminded me of well-manicured golf course fairways. There was a spider's web of pathways joining the houses, which were respectfully distanced from each other with no sign of property divisions or fences. They really seemed to be a united people with the rare ability to live in harmony. The houses were all surrounded by shade trees, most bearing fruit like mango and *craboo*, and with the river close by it was delightfully cool. Nicodemus's wife and daughters were busying themselves with supper inside a wild-cane-and-palmetto thatched roofed structure. The logs were creating some nice-looking coals under the tin lid of the mud stove and there was a pot of beans boiling and a larger pot next to it that seemed to be ready for the rooster whose neck one of the sons had just wrung with a dexterous twist of his muscular wrist. The two daughters, both with sleeping babies strapped to their backs, were slapping some corn tortillas into shape, these being my favourite using freshly milled corn instead of the packaged maize flour. I smiled at one of the daughters as she eyed me curiously and then returned a toothless grin. Most of the young women's husbands were on the banks with other boats and had left them to pool resources or move in with parents or in-laws until they got back. As night fell, the *fifi* lamps were lit and in the distance I could hear the thudding of a generator, probably at the Red Cross station.

The meal was simple yet wholesome and Nicodemus said grace which, although I understood but half, I could tell was sincere and I was indeed thankful for a safe passage over from the islands and for having accomplished my tasks that day without any setbacks. I knew by now that Zarco or Captain Robert (who was probably coming alive by then) had called Elly on the single sideband radio to let her know that we had arrived and that she would have informed our families. There was no table and we all sat on *petates*, or straw mats, cross-legged or seated leaning up against the wall. While we began our meal, country music played from a tape recorder somewhere, probably at the *chicha* bar where the divers were blowing their advances on home-brewed liquor.

After the meal I went outside for a bucket bath in a canvas cubicle that housed a long-drop toilet and wood-planked floor that served as the bathing area. I took my towel and fresh shorts and a T-shirt to change there since it was now dark outside and I would not risk the shame of exposing myself in front of Nicodemus's family. There were no rooms per se inside his house. It was just one open room so sleeping arrangements were simple— each one to his own *petate* and not many pillows to go 'round. Nicodemus and his wife had a thin mattress that they rolled out at night in one of the corners. I was given a *petate* and used my clothes sack for a pillow. It wasn't long before the *fifis* were blown out and everyone was snoring and I gazed at the stars in a magnificently clear sky through the open window and listened to the crickets and cicadas before my day too was done.

The next one started early with the pink glow of sunrise peeking through the trees from the eastern horizon, roosters crowing, dogs barking, and pots and pans clanging while breakfast was being prepared. At 6:00, Abel came over with Filiberto and we smoked the first Royal of the day after a breakfast of maize porridge called *atol* and tortillas. We gathered up our things and made for the beach for the hundred-yard paddle out to the boat. We were lucky it was calm with just small breakers, and we were on board in no time.

I was happy to find Robert up and looking sharp. He was on his desk in the wheelhouse looking over his charts that had little jottings he had made over the years noting the places he had fished and what the catch was. I say fishing but it wasn't fishing in the conventional sense for scale fish using lines or nets. No, it was the technique of finding an area where conch or lobster were known to be, anchoring the boat, and sending the dories out with the divers descending to seamounts, some shallow, others deep. Each diver was equipped with nothing more than flippers, a mask, a backpack to hold the tank (no buoyancy compensator or BC), a regulator, a sack to place the conch in, a chipping hammer to break the conch underwater, and a simple cutlery knife to prise the conch out of the shell. This was tiring work mostly done at sixty to ninety feet below, hitting the conch shell in the exact spot—and there *was* an exact spot which I had also been taught by my brothers in St. Helene—with the knife separating the white tip of flesh that attached the conch to the inside of the shell and with the other hand grabbing the long fingernail of the conch inside its large pink mouth, pulling it out and popping it into the sack. One tank at sixty feet would last an hour for an experienced diver, and if we were on top of the conch he could fill the sack with around forty to fifty conchs. An inexperienced diver who couldn't control his breathing would breathe like he was on land and within thirty minutes would be out of air with maybe just ten conchs. This was another thing—there was no depth or pressure gauge, so a diver would rely on listening to the tank ring after every breath which would indicate that the air was down to its last. Another sign was when the air had to be sucked out of the tank instead of just floating into your lungs at the slightest hint of inhalation as was normal, but this was pushing it and when this happened it was time to make the ascent while harnessing the panic and making damned sure your bubbles floated up faster than you did to make sure you didn't get an embolism. The tragedy of this type of diving was that this happened often and was why many *Waiknas* were paraplegics, including Zarco's twin.

Zarco and Johnny were in the wheelhouse together with the Captain, who actually looked pleased to see me. I knew this because he greeted me with "you damned Limey, I thought those *Waikna* girls had swallowed you up!" It looked like they were planning another Rosalind Bank run where we had hit them the previous trip and I asked him jokingly if he thought he was going to catch the same conchs we caught last trip. This precipitated much mirth from all present, including Robert's growling laugh, always followed by a coughing fit. The Captain was back with us and it gave us hope.

Around midday, the divers started to arrive in dribs and drabs with the tangible odour of stale overnight booze. They arrived with their dories and their sacks of clothing; strangely, none had suitcases, duffle bags, or hold-alls just like us, the crew. The dories were hauled on board and placed on the gunwales on either side of the back deck, side by side, giving the back deck the look of type of a rectangular sunflower with brown instead of yellow petals. At nights, to escape the heat of the crew bunks in the bow and the plywood bunk area above the wheelhouse, the divers and dory men would sleep inside the dorys with their pieces of foam.

Robert set the course for Rosalind some 480 kilometers away. If we left at 2:00 after lunch that day, we reasoned, we would be there by late afternoon the following day and ready to dive the day after that. The Captain and Zarco would have first watch until midnight and then Johnny, Abel, and I would take the wheel and engine room watch until 0600. Seas were calm, which bode well for our luck, and we weighed anchor and headed east.

While underway during daylight hours, two 150-pound test lines were set out at the back in the hopes a kingfish or tuna would grab it. Johnny prepared the bait using a sliver of barracuda belly with a piece of onion sack over it to give it some colour. Just before dusk we hit a big king mackerel and there was whooping and hollering from everyone on the back while Zarco dropped the revs down a bit so the fish could be hauled on board. This together with the *Journey cakes* or Johnny Cakes that Dan had been baking with his assistant cook, Cesar Trapp, whom we had picked up at Patuca, was to be supper. After supper and my smoke, I filled up my enamel mug from the day tank, cleaned my teeth, and laid down on my bunk in the galley. While Dan had the light on, I read a passage from my small Gideon's Bible that I always brought with me on the banks. I opened it up to the page where I kept the

58

pressed four-leaf clover that Mother had given me years before. Ezekiel 47, verse 10, *"and it will come about that fishermen will stand beside it: from Engedi to Eneglaim there will be a place for the spreading of nets. Their fish will be according to their kinds, like the fish of the Great Sea, very many."*

The passage between ports and banks was always exciting in a mundane sort of way, hundreds of kilometers of wide-open ocean interrupted now and again by a large fish on the end of our lines or large tankers or container ships that even sounded their horns when they passed close enough. It was a pleasant passage, seas under ten knots and the divers on the back deck playing cards, Cassino being the preferred game. Shrieks of laughter mixed with shouts of joy and much jabbering in Miskito marked the end of each game. Dan and Cesar Trapp kept us in meals like clockwork, and if you needed coffee it was there. We were mostly left alone with our thoughts, looking out to sea and breathing the salt air and as Joseph Conrad wrote, *"the sea perhaps because of its saltiness toughens the outside but sweetens the kernel of its servant's soul."* This was true in my case, and I suspect for many of those on *The Gladiator* as we punched eastward unto an uncertain near future. *Waiknas* looked out to sea alone, pensively, at all hours of the night. I also found myself alone for hours at a time since I was always given the midnight-to-dawn wheel watch. Time to reflect on how I would be as a father to my unborn child, how I could be better husband. I found myself bored in my marriage with nothing in common with my wife and tending to get out of the house more regularly, spending time with a rough crowd drinking and not coming back until early morning to find her awake and worried about me, poor thing. I thought a lot about my life in the islands; I was still young and could go back and start a career and a life in England, but something kept me there, compelled me to stay. Times were tough and money was scarce, but we made it somehow and I "felt in my water," as I heard the Bantu in Africa often say, that one day life would be easier and more comfortable.

We neared Rosalind at dusk as a sliver of red sun was slowly edging below the quicksand of the horizon. Rosalind Bank was a huge, featureless bank with no cays or breaking reefs and some one hundred kilometers long. It was located halfway between Patuca and Jamaica and on the very northeast corner of the shelf that was known to us as *The Banks* and extended three hundred kilometers from the mouth of the Rio Coco. After a short while motoring slowly and looking at the chart and the Loran, we found the spot the Captain was looking for, slightly east of the bank's shallowest point which was around sixty feet and the anchor was weighed noisily. Supper was on the go and Abel and Johnny already had the compressors going pumping tanks three at a time inside a plastic barrel full of water to keep them cool. Each tank with the Bauer K-15 would take ten minutes to fill, so they wanted to get a head start to be able to give each dory three tanks for the morning session. As dories came in the next day, we would receive the empty tanks and fill them up as quickly as possible to give the divers a swift turnaround. The secret was to make sure that the diesel engine powering the compressor's exhaust was well distanced from the air intake for the compressor; if it wasn't, the tank would be filled with a high level of carbon monoxide and we would poison the divers. That night before the first day of diving, Nicodemus had a church service and they sang some hymns in Miskito that I recognized the tunes to—one of them was "How Great Thou Art"—and I sang along with them in English.

The morning gave us choppier seas than we had seen in previous days. To a man, everyone was up at 4:00 racking up the equipment, checking regulators, adjusting backpacks, fitting masks and flippers. The crew were busying themselves stacking tanks and readying the compressors for the long day ahead. As dawn broke, everyone was lining up at the galley ready for breakfast, which to no one's surprise was a hard Johnny cake and a mug full of Cream of Wheat loaded with sugar and powdered milk. It was the easiest for Dan and Oscar Trapp to prepare quickly for forty men. The crew generally cooked their own after the divers had left and Dan always cooked breakfast especially for the Captain.

As I was stacking tanks in just a pair of cut-off jeans, I glanced forward and caught a glimpse of the Captain standing on the top step of the wheelhouse with his foot up on the railing, a mug of coffee in his hand and a smoke in his mouth. He, too, was bareback and he was looking down at me, grinning, with the sun beginning to peek over the horizon in all its pink splendour. It wasn't a mocking grin he gave me; it seemed more like a grin of admiration for what I was doing in another country, living an adventurous life and doing as everyone else did, supporting a family and making a living. He was a kindred spirit. We liked each other and I suppose it was conceited of me at the time to believe that he felt pride in what he had been able to teach me.

Rosalind was the most unimpressive bank I had been to. It had no cays like Serranilla or breaking reefs like Quita Sueño. It was all just a lighter blue than the deep sea we had crossed to get there. The shallowest part was a deep turquoise since the whole bank had just a sandy sea floor with very few coral formations that were small at that. Serranilla Bank, a former atoll and now a submerged reef just south of where we were on Rosalind, was my favourite. I once spent a week there as a diver and with my diving partner at the time explored some of the small islets that were sparsely vegetated with bushes and some trees. The desolation of hearing the wind whistling through the bushes and shrubs punctuated by the quack of boobies and chuckle of gulls was soothing, as if we belonged there always. We had found a nest full of turtle eggs and ate a handful between us, sitting on the most beautiful white sand beach looking over the purest crystal-clear turquoise water I had ever been privileged to witness. Being my mother's son, I took a handful of colourful shells from the beach, selected the best, and put them in my pocket to remember that day in that most idyllic of places.

At our anchor on Rosalind the dories started to trickle back around 10:00. The catches with three tanks were meagre and the stories were the same. Freshly broken shells littered the sea floor; someone had beaten us to a big herd of conch and cleaned up. Most likely *The Pioneer*, a hand-built boat from Bonacca that had passed through Patuca picking up divers while we were fiddling around getting *The Gladiator* ready. At noon, the Captain made the call to head ten kilometers north to a spot he had done well at a few years back, and the divers were in the water by 2:00. The same result—cleaned out broken shells everywhere. This was of concern to our Captain because every time we moved the boat we were burning diesel that had been calculated to the last drop and moving around a bank that was a hundred kilometers long became expensive. That night after supper we gathered around the chart and he announced that we would make one last attempt on Rosalind in an area on the southeast that was deep, ninety to 120 feet. This meant that each diver would probably only be able to dive four tanks a day instead of six. He punched in the waypoint on the Loran and said we would move at 3:00 a.m. to be there at dawn.

For once I didn't have the graveyard watch, which the Captain took, probably because his worries and creeping self-doubt about losing his own shrewd abilities as a captain were keeping him awake at night. I was up together with everyone else on board right before dawn, busying ourselves for the day that lay ahead. Everyone had hope and faith in our skipper to place us right on top of the conchs, and we were imagining what we would do with all of our money. So eager to get in the water to see what was there for us below that a dory even got going without breakfast, just taking three hard Johnny cakes with their canteen of water and pack of smokes. Smokes and Andrews Salts, or *Sal Andrews*—the bane of my existence on the boat since I was stores keeper. *"Miriki, gimme one pack cigaret... Miriki, gimme one Sal Andrew, wini saura (I feel bad)."* To which I would smile and say, *"Man siknes brisma (are you sick)?"* It was a pantomime repeated each day, morning and evening. They paid for the cigarettes and it was deducted after the end of each trip, but the Andrews Salts were free and they liked the taste and guzzled them down as fast as they could connive their way into convincing me to dole them out.

By 7:00 all dories were overboard, spread out on the ocean and organized so that none would encroach on the next man's patch. It was choppy and therefore difficult for the dorymen, who had to paddle harder to keep up and see the bubbles of their divers ninety feet below. The dories were spread out as far as the eye could see around the boat, and we started to see divers surfacing far away from their dories and much singsong cursing was going on between doryman and diver. A strong squall lasting twenty minutes made down around midmorning, which wasn't felt by the divers below but the dorymen who couldn't abandon their divers were having a wretched time of it.

Right after the passing of the squall, a young diver called Ruben was standing up in his dory shouting, "Shark! Shark!" so that everyone could get out of the water. It was a big tiger shark that ripped Ruben's sack of conch out of his hand while he held it out in front of him as he surfaced, lest he get mauled. Johnny rushed for the heavy towing line we used and asked Dan for a piece of meat, which he placed on the hook and threw overboard as bait to draw the shark in and catch it before he terrorized the divers and caused a bloodbath. By its rushing movements we knew it was desperate and very hungry, much like all of us. It got close to the boat, sensing the blood, and darted underneath from bow to stern, probing and sensing the meat with each pass. It got closer and closer as everyone on board watched until it finally gave in to curiosity and hunger and with a sideways shuffle and half-upward roll of its large, striped frame lunged at the hook and immediately realized it had made a greedy mistake and made a run for the deep. It was just as well, and indeed a miracle in itself that Johnny, despite the perpetual ganja fog that filled his brain, had the presence of mind to grab the slack of the 150-pound test nylon fishing line and tie it off on one of the steel struts on the outrigger. A little while after that, the line came tight and made a sound like a high-pitched whine as the wind passed across it. Everyone on board was now watching and hoping that the line would hold fast. The shark was writhing in anger, and we could see its white underbelly thrashing and rolling in the depths below, trying to shake the large Norwegian hook loose—not knowing in its savage ignorance that the more it struggled the deeper the hook sank into its flesh. The Captain was out on the back deck with us by then and with his gravelly voice barked, "Don't worry, he'll get tired in a bit and we'll pull him aboard and cut his ass up."

It took about forty-five minutes of the ebb and flow, giving it slack only for us to take it right back up again, for the shark to get tired and for the line to gradually get slack so that we could begin pulling it upwards for the last time. It was about ten feet from the boat, so close we could see its fearful, enraged eye. It nodded bullishly, attempting to dart for the deep and escape its fate, but when it did Johnny was ready. He took in a bite on the outrigger and when the shark relaxed, we all took in the slack quickly, its energy and will to live finally drained. By now all the divers had used up their tanks and were ready to come in for the midday break but were keeping their distance because they could see the commotion onboard, although they were unsure of the cause. We brought it alongside the boat, watching as it just moved its tailfin from side to side listlessly, resigned to its fate. Abel slipped a black rope noose over its tail and we hoisted it up. It was a large female, a good thirteen to fourteen feet in length and weighing all of five hundred pounds. She was out of the water and not moving and it wasn't long before she suffocated to death.

On the back deck we slit her belly open to find she was full of young. This explained why she was so determined, desperate, and hungry. We had invaded her space and slaughtered her and deprived her unborn of life. We were the cruel interlopers, unwelcomed, destroying and interfering with nature wherever we decided. Seafarers are superstitious and random acts of cruelty like killing an albatross or slaughtering a pregnant shark left an uneasiness among us, expecting ill fortune to follow afterwards. The shark was cut up in pieces and salted by most to take home what we didn't eat on board. The oil was claimed by one of the divers since it was a sought-after medicine for all sorts of ailments. The jaw was cut out as a souvenir. The fins were cut off and dried to be sold.

Both morning and afternoon sessions were disappointing for the divers. On a good conch sea floor such as Rosalind, divers could expect to bring in fifty pounds in a day, but it was slim pickings with lots of empty shells and the most any of them brought in was twenty pounds; the total for for all dories that day was three hundred pounds. The disappointment and concern was etched on everyone's faces but we kept our hopes up as I checked everyone's tally into my little children's exercise book where I had made a neat little table on each page for each day and where I also kept a log of the day's events. That day's entry just read "shark killed" since it was too unsettling to remember and elaborate on.

After supper the Captain gathered the crew together in the wheelhouse over coffee to discuss where to try next. We discussed trying the very southern edge of Rosalind, but we knew that two boats from Jonesville with good divers had gone ahead of us, and that the young Captain Indio on *The Apollo* was proving to be an astute fisherman with a knack for finding product.

"I say we haul our asses to Alice Shoal," said Robert.

"It's deep there, Cap," said Zarco. It was deep indeed, maybe forty feet at its shallowest and sixteen miles wide, but the hardest thing to deal with for divers was the currents. We weren't in Honduran waters, but this wasn't Nicaragua either, and the Jamaican and Colombian coast guards and navies were too far away to be bothered. So we travelled further east to Alice Shoal to be ready to dive again in the morning. It was becoming a disappointing routine of moving location at night and diving with slim pickings during the day, slowly eating away at our fuel supply.

We knocked out two unremarkable days on Alice Shoal and dived the *Waiknas* as much as we dared without risking any of them getting bent. The closest decompression chamber was two days away, by which time damage to any human would be irreversible. Twelve hundred pounds was the best we could do and then we were back to the skipper's charts full of jottings. Captain Robert had remained upbeat during this poor run of fortune and actually seemed to be enjoying his freedom from the abusive life he had been living for the past months on shore; he was gaining colour and eating regularly. It seemed of little consequence to him that we had less than two thousand pounds of conch after four full days of diving and a week since we had left home, having travelled several hundred kilometers of ocean.

Each night we would listen in to the single sideband to the chatter from other fishing boats to hear of their fortunes, but mostly they spoke in riddles and so it was difficult to decipher how they were doing. Listening and reading between the lines, it seemed that Captain Lalman from Jonesville had enjoyed a few good days on Serranilla then Serrana, so it didn't make much sense going back in that direction. With our hearts in our mouths, we were beginning to have to face the inevitable. Our options were fast being whittled down to Quita Sueno Bank and, God forbid, having a run at Nicaragua. It was decided to set a course southwest for Quita Sueno, which was in Colombian territory 110 kilometers north-northeast of Providencia although curiously it was closer to Nicaragua and Honduras.

An overnight passage again, with a following wind of around ten knots, and I wasn't by myself in the wheelhouse. Robert had brought a bag of weed with him, probably hidden away in a place known only to him and Johnny, and they were rolling and smoking while me and Abel listened in, Zarco pensive at the wheel. Filiberto and Nicodemus sat on the top steps to the wheelhouse, and even Oscar Trapp and One-Eyed Dan joined us with their tin mugs full of sweet black coffee. There was a crescent moon on the wane and the universe of stars was as clear as I had only seen in Africa. I stepped out on the back deck to escape the worst of the weed smoke and looked back at the sky where we had come from, at the Big and Little Dippers with the North Star, Polaris at the very tip of its panhandle. Looking at a clear night sky considering that all the stars were suns was always hard for me to get my head around, to think that the starlight that I was seeing was light that had been emitted when dinosaurs roamed earth. I had Vaughan Williams' *Fantasia on a Theme* by Thomas Tallis playing in my head and found myself humming it with a certain sense of nostalgia that I always had when I heard it. It reminded me of the sea when I was away from it and now it reminded me of home where my pregnant wife was, but also of my mother who had no idea at that point where I was.

At dawn we could make out the dark shape of the lighthouse on the northern tip off the reef and the wreck that lay just south of it. Quita Sueno was so called because it was a notably rough area with a long reef some forty miles long, dotted with wrecks of vessels that had run afoul of the reef that rises up in the middle of nowhere. Quita Sueno in Spanish means "takes away sleep." It was to be a lobster dive, not conch this time. The reef here was rich with healthy brain and elkhorn coral where pockets of big lobsters were to be found given the right cycle of the moon and tides. As the sun rose, we could make out the shades of turquoise blues interspersed with the browns, yellows, and tans of the corals below the surface that we had missed so much and that reminded us of home. The Captain had a smoke dangling from the corner of his mouth, bareback and barefoot with his Greek fisherman's cap on. He wore a grin—or was it a smirk?—on his face that gave us some hope, as if he knew something we didn't. Johnny had pulled out a tape recorder the night before during their weed session and he was playing Robert's's favourite tune, which became mine also since I tried to emulate him in everything. It was Josey Wales' "Let Go Mi Hand":

"I went to a dance down in Clarendon... me and a big fat ting named Pam... when I reached, to the dance hall, the gateman hold up on me woman's hand... one box me give I in him blasted face... you love brag and you love show off, you move 'round like a shovelmouth shark... put me neck 'pon a block and even chop it off, put it in a wheelbarrow, fling it down a wharf..."

And when it got to that part that we knew all too well, we all chanted together with him, *"mi duppy come back and it still a laugh,"* which he always sang with a relish while shuffling and moving his hips as if in the Casa Grande Dancehall in Pandy Town. It was a happy time, dancing and singing with the seas beginning to calm as he took us around the northern point of the reef to the sheltered west side where we anchored.

It was to be freediving, no tanks, since the reef was shallow and that meant they could stay out as long as they could handle it. The lobsters were caught using fishing hooks wrapped to a piece of metal rod using stainless steel wire with the barb filed off. The diver would deftly run the hook through the surface of the sand below the breastplate of the lobster. Once he knew that the point of the hook was underneath the fleshy part of the tail—ideally the weak spot between tail and thorax—he would lift up and pull the rod sharply towards him, hooking the lobster, which would be killed by jabbing it in the chest with the filed-down point on the opposite end of the hookstick. An experienced diver could find a rock hole or ledge with four or five big ones, *hairy toes*, and hook and kill them all one after the other with clinical efficiency within a minute. They had to learn to do this because when the lobsters sensed they were being attacked they would back up deep into their hideouts and nothing would get them out, not even a moray eel. I enjoyed being in shallow water and got overboard myself to nail on the sheets of tarred plywood over the leaking planks. The job had been overdue since we left port, and I was helped by Johnny and Abel who had no tanks to pump. Even in the water Abel wore full-length jeans so we wouldn't see his scars.

The divers returned in drips and drabs at midday for lunch and brought their meager catch with them. Most of the holes were empty with signs of broken whips and even shed lobster suits, indicating that someone had been there just days before and the moon was the shedding moon for lobsters. "*Labsta apu,*" we heard the divers repeat dejectedly. We were there for two days and, although most of the divers were out from dawn to nighttime scouring the best part of the reef, the best the boat could scrape together was three hundred pounds, three miserable boxes.

"That's all we need to buy some diesel from Forch," reasoned the skipper that evening, sipping on his molasses-thick coffee and the perpetual smoke on the go. Forch Merren was a Bonnacian from Guanaja who traded the fishing banks from San Andres to Jamaica and the Cayman Islands, buying conch, lobster, and fish for cash or trading for fuel or other goods and then turning around and selling to brokers in Cayman and Jamaica. His vessel was an old oilfield supply boat, *The Hard Way*, and when he was asked how he came about that name he would say, "I got it the hard way," which meant he had worked hard as a merchant seaman in America to buy it in an auction in Bayou La Batre.

"Hardway, Hardway, Hardway, this is *The Gladiator*, you read me? Captain Forch? Come back." Robert's gravelly voice always punctuated his SSB calls with commentary of what we were going to do as if thinking aloud. "Sep my Christ" was his favourite kick-off. "We'll get our fuel from Forch and head over to Martinez Reefs and finish the trip on a high, you bunch of pussies." This is what we didn't want to hear. Martinez Reefs, Nicaraguan waters below the fifteen-degrees latitude line where the Rio Coco separated Honduras and Nicaragua. The Sandinista Navy base at Puerto Cabezas was just fifty miles away and if alerted to any Honduran-flagged fishing vessel they would be out after us in a flash. A fishing vessel from Oakridge, *The Morning Mist*, and its crew had been caught a few years previously and spent months in jail and the boat never made it back. It was literally tempting fate for us on this salt-luck trip to venture into Nicaragua. Everything had gone wrong so far and this would be the bitter end. I had a million dark thoughts going through my head at that point, imagining what my pregnant wife would do to manage with me gone and wondering how my parents would know what had happened were we to be caught. No one was smiling and there was silence in the wheelhouse, save for the chattering and shrieking of the divers who were coming in after the afternoon session with their meager catches.

The atmosphere of concern was soon broken by the crackle and hiss of the SSB and Forch on *The Hard Way* calling us. "*Gladiator, Gladiator, Gladiator, this is the Hard Way, come in, Captain Robert.*" He was on his way from Serrana Bank en route to Providencia and would turn back to Quita Sueño if we had at least twenty-five boxes of lobster—which we didn't, but once he was there what could he do? He would be with us by morning. Once *The Hard Way* was up alongside us the next day, we had the tires we used for fenders over the side and made ready to receive her lines. We were inside the reef in about twenty feet of white water, so it was calm. Johnny and Zarco went down into the cold room and started handing up the bags of lobster up to a few divers who passed them over to be weighed on *The Hard Way*. Being the checker, I went on board to witness the weighing. Robert was already on the bridge in the skipper's quarters negotiating with Captain Forch. The best we could do was twenty boxes, two thousand pounds, which at forty lempiras a pound was eighty thousand lempiras. After paying the divers and crew, the skipper had half of that to get fueled and victualed.

Marvill Merren, Forch's brother (who was called *Balin* because his name was Marvill which sounded like "marble" which was *balin* in Spanish) was the Chief Engineer on *The Hard Way* and had met me a year previously and made pleasant conversation and told me a few yarns about the history of Guanaja over a cup of coffee and hot buttered toast with Marmite, which was a luxury in those parts. He was working the scales with me and when we had finished, he called me aside and told me to wait while he went to his cabin. He came back and presented me with a jar of Marmite and was proud to tell me that he had bought it in Georgetown, Grand Cayman a while after our last encounter because when he saw it he thought of me and had been carrying it around with him ever since in the hopes that he would meet me again. He did, that day, and in this act of kindness brought a joy to my day and an encouragement before what I was expecting to be a bad day the following day. Impulsively I scribbled down my mother's name and phone number on a piece of paper I tore from my exercise book where I kept my checkings and journal and asked that if he heard of some misfortune happening to our boat that he call my mother when he got to Bonacca or Georgetown. This kindred spirit looked me in the eye knowingly and took the paper slip.

After Robert and Forch had negotiated we loaded fuel and cut *The Hard Way* loose. We left after a supper of flitter and fried fish around 8:00 p.m. It was a stealth mission and we had to arrive at dawn and shove the dories off quickly; time was of the essence. We would turn off all lights on the passage over, even the running lights. We couldn't alert the Sandinistas to our presence. No one was able to sleep and we were all in the wheel house; Johnny and Robert, showing rare self-control, limited themselves to just the one joint. Everyone knew we had to be on our best the next day. The Captain briefed us that night that in case the Navy were alerted and we had to get away in a hurry, our fallback would be to cut one of the butane tanks from its stand and take it down it into the engine room, put the hose into the air filter housing and open the valve to boost the RPMs of the CAT main engine with the butane. We could only do this for thirty minutes max for fear of breaking the engine (crankshaft or connecting rod catastrophe).

We arrived at the Martinez Reefs which were north of the Miskito Cays just as the sky was pinking, and Robert astutely positioned *The Gladiator* on the north side of the reef to keep it between us and Puerto Cabezas, the direction they would come from. We didn't weigh anchor, thinking it would waste too much time to pull it up in the event we needed a quick getaway. We would just keep the boat hovering. The divers had eaten in the dark a little before we arrived and at daybreak the skipper had put us right on the north end of the whole Miskito Cays, the Martinez Reefs bank strategically blocking us off from any approaching Navy patrol boats that would come in from the main Sandinista Naval base at Puerto Cabezas. He had done this before on his first boat, *The Ronnie Mc.*, and so this gave me some comfort since we were poaching.

The reefs were in no way impressive compared to the beauty of places we had been. Dark, muddy, and very shallow with interspersed hints of blues and whites. The divers had been told to keep their dories close by and not roam too far in case we had an alert from the Navy and had to flee. By 9:00 we knew it was going well. We could see the divers from the boat as they were throwing in handfuls of lobsters, and we could hear their shrieks of joy as they paddled to the next patch. The lobsters were all on the shallow, on the *dry reef* as islanders would say. They all came in at midday for a bite and smokes but were anxious to get back since we knew we couldn't overnight there.

At mid-afternoon Zarco, who had spent most of the day perched on the tip of the upright mainmast as a lookout with a large straw hat for the sun, shouted down to the Captain that he could see a wake and an exhaust plume coming rapidly from the southeast straight towards us. We all looked in that direction and, given that the horizon was four kilometers away, we didn't have much time to get the divers onboard. But they had already seen what we had and were all paddling furiously towards us. "Get the butane tank down in the engine room!" the skipper barked at me. "But don't open it until I tell you."

We had to leave some of the dories behind since we had no time to pull them on board, but all the catch was aboard and we would weigh later if indeed we got out of this. Adrenaline was coursing through everyone's veins, all focused on the getaway. We were fortunate that boat's position was in a very shallow area that was situated in such a way that there was nothing but reef and a few narrow channels between us and the Sandinistas. Negotiating the channels would slow them down and allow us to make a break, but they had a machine gun mounted on the front of their vessel and we didn't. "Alright boys, open up the butane tank." Robert had a smirk on his face as he told us to do it. He was really grooving on it all and was even singing that part of the Josey Wales song, "mi duppy come back and me a still a laugh!"

Johnny and I placed the hose from the butane tank into the housing and opened the valve, forcing the engine to RPMs it had never been to before and wasn't designed for. We had thirty minutes maximum.

It was at the moment when the Sandinista patrol boat captain realized that our captain, Robert McNab (of British blood, whose descendants centuries before him had similarly outwitted the Spanish Armada) was now getting away from him and heading north the thirty-odd kilometers to Honduran waters and the protection of Alligator Reef that he decided to open fire and intimidate us. The machine gun started thumping away and we heard it before we saw the trail of red-hot heat rounds drifting towards us in a slow arc. They were seeking us, and I knew that behind every heat round we could see there were two we could not. The communists didn't have.50-caliber weapons, but they had something better, the 14.5 mm which was equivalent to.57-caliber and this was what they were bringing to bear on us as the *Waikna* divers were all prostrate on the back deck, praying and singing hymns.

During combat, real time in seconds would seem like hours, and at one point Zarco, who had bravely stayed up on the mast not as lookout but as a guide for Robert through the maze of coral reefs, fell down from the top as one of the Sandinista rounds hit the mast a foot below where he had one of his hands, leaving a hole the size of a baseball. He most likely fell from the impact of the round hitting the metal mainmast, not out of fear, and he hit the deck with a sickening thump like a sack of beans. He remained motionless for what must have been a minute. I was at the opening down into the engine room, having come up from securing the butane tank with Johnny when I saw Zarco fall. By instinct I checked his vital signs which I really couldn't detect quite honestly, but it didn't matter because as I pressed two fingers into his carotid artery feeling for a pulse, he began crawling like an iguana felled from a tree down into the engine room. His face was still blue from being winded.

"It's okay, Zarco, we're going to be all right," I reassured him. "English, bring me glass water," was all he could manage, his eyes as big as saucers. The gunfire began to subside in the distance as the Sandinistas realized they had been outdone that day and Robert bellowed at us to unhook the tank "before we roast this fucking CAT through the hull!" Whoops of joy and hugs swept through the crew as we got close to the fifteen-degrees latitude line marked by the mouth of the Rio Coco.

Savannah Cay was a small cay on a reef system that included Alligator Reef to the south and Half Moon Reef to the north, and although it belonged to Honduras it was inhabited by Jamaicans who, to a man, were Rastafarians who fished the surrounding waters with traps or *fishpots*. They used fiberglass catboats or pangas and were very skilled at it. This is where we arrived to anchor that evening after our narrow escape. We could have made it to Patuca that night, but the mood was festive and it was almost as if we were at the end of a successful trip even though it had been severely shortened and our catch was dismal. But the euphoria of freedom and life after an adrenaline high overshadowed the looming crises and difficulties we all faced in our own private lives.

We had made friends in the past with the Jamaicans, and they always had a steady supply of weed which Robert, Johnny, and a few of the divers were after. The usual bargain was a sack of dried *Irish moss* for a small Milex powdered milk tin full of the *Red Eye Boom* as they called it. Irish sea moss was a delicacy in a porridge for the Jamaicans and had medicinal qualities and being fishermen who didn't dive, they were always game. They could handle themselves in Miskito because they used to make a run to Kruta on the Miskito Coast once a month for basic supplies in their catboats; some of them had traditionally built, toothless girlfriends there. There were six of them, all orthodox Rastafarians, and my favourite was Moses who had his dreads down to his ankle but most of the time held it tied up in an old white T-shirt. He was a good listener and imparted wisdom. God only knows how old he was.

That night we went to the Cay, several dories, and we had a bonfire with roasted snapper, lobster, and now-ripe *filipitos* we had brought from onboard the boat. The divers got their share of the weed and had a gallon of *Chicha Levadura* they had been saving for the end of the trip. The Captain was euphoric after having led us out of the jaws of a certain demise and seemed to have gained a new lease on life with it. He always tried to talk like the Jamaicans when we met up with them and his face glowed when Moses, the leader, would call him "Captain sah." It was another happy time. There was a broad swath of moonlight across the open sea and small wavelets caressed the shore with an even rhythm. There was a heady aroma of burning dried buttonwood, marijuana, seaweed, and body odour. Moses was sitting next to me on an upturned dory.

"Lion." He had always called me this and I felt chuffed that he did. "Bob Marley always said that the greatness of a man is not in how much wealth he acquires, but in his integrity and his ability to affect those around him positively. One day unah a do tings back yard datta help yah breda man." Moses wasn't looking at me when he said this; his glazed, bloodshot eyes were staring into the coals and flames as if in a trance.

It is a testament to the fickleness of humans that after a crisis, a flurry of foxhole prayers, and numerous pledges to do better before the Almighty, we are quick to forget. Although we had only been gone ten days, it seemed like years since we had left our homes. The divers were heading back to the lush riverside of Patuca with their yard fowl and gleeful, grubby-faced children and toothless wives to await the next trip while farming and fishing. The crew, all of us with our own dilemmas and pressures, would have to see how we could juggle things around and hustle to pay some of our bills here, extend credit there. Robert not only had bills overflowing, he had a fierce dragon within that he had to slay; if he didn't, his world would unravel. In the end he would keep on the straight and narrow for the two weeks it took to get the boat ready on a type of marijuana maintenance program, no rum. I stayed put at home, mainly because there was no money to drink, which of course my wife loved. My first child, my lovely little daughter with dimples, was born in this time and gave me more reason to stay at home instead of "walking 'bout" as my wife called it.

The follow-up trip was a success, despite me having a serious altercation with Matthias where I nearly knocked his block off and spent a night in a wild cane jail. We hit a large herd of conch on North Rosalind and then cleaned up on Serranilla and Bajo Nuevo and ended up with four hundred boxes after only three weeks. Robert was able to come current with the bank, pay the supply house. We were all able to pay off our personal debts and have some money for our pockets and that's where we forgot our pledges and our prayers from the first trip. Robert got worse and Johnny followed close behind. Zarco jumped ship and started working with another boat due to Robert's instability. I decided to take a job as a welder on the dock at the fish plant, and a few months later on another boat as compressorman to escape my own demons. Abel left for Iriona to fish and farm and One-Eyed Dan drank himself to death in Bonacca.

All the lessons learned during our times of struggle—the humility of the *Waiknas*, the kindness from *Balin*, bravery in the face of danger from Zarco and Robert—were lost from us for a season but they all came back to us eventually and that is what inspired us inevitably to clean up our acts and broaden our horizons. We were able to enjoy successes. Robert, clean and sober, eventually landed a job as a captain on a seismographic vessel in the Gulf of Mexico and started enjoying life with a sober head. I went through the wringer, made the same mistakes as the Captain, following in his self-destructive footsteps, destroyed a family but came out of the other side sober and landing a steady job. Little did I know that day as I sat on that mangrove root that this was just a beginning.

Espejito

I had to go to the windfarm to look at some scrap that had been left behind and abandoned by a contractor, and also to inform the manager and two of his key employees, an electrician and a mechanic, of their pay raises and to congratulate them on doing a good job. They had recently repaired ten turbines after a terrible lightning storm six months back. David and Geovanny were good men, self-taught from humble families. Their boss Gustavo, my friend of twenty-five years, was in between marriages trying to put substance abuse behind him and I had given him the job he needed to get his life back on track. Older than me by eight years, we had worked together years ago for the same company in different guises, he as the diesel plant manager and me as the line supervisor. The fact that we had spent Hurricane Mitch sleeping on flattened-out cardboard boxes on the planthouse floor, eating nothing but cocktail sausages and *Club Sociales* soda biscuits in darkness with the wind howling outside, listening to the dreadful news from the mainland, forged our friendship. His sense of humour complemented mine and he was constantly mocking my Spanish pronunciation. He had not let me down, had seized the opportunity with both hands and made a success of the facility, leaving his demons behind.

The windfarm itself was something that I took pride in since I had built it together with a group of contractors I trusted after the first contractor had walked with $2 million of our money. It was hard work, though, and there were many heated moments and several bridges burned along the way. So, at the same time, just being there always brought back the unpleasant memories that shadowed the pride I felt in the accomplishment of its construction. To wit, I only went there when it was completely necessary. This time I had been convinced by Gustavo that my presence would mean a great deal to the troops, especially if it meant news of a pay raise, modest as it was. I was somewhat of a legend within our organization, I would have liked to think, in much the same way the big fish relishes in being the largest in the small pond and using this ruse Gustavo coaxed me into the visit that day.

We had a look at the scrap, which consisted of a huge metal funnel once used for mixing the aggregate to form the huge concrete bases for the towers. There were also two containers used by my close friend poor Guy Muller as bodegas; sadly, after his passing not even his son came and picked them up or cared for them. We decided that we couldn't use them, the rust having beaten us to it. We drove up to the highest hill where the first turbine was put in service and had a look at the grass being chopped, yes, chopped, not mowed. Gustavo showed me the small plantation being started by some of the guards, some corn that was coming on nicely and some promising-looking cassava.

Back to the office, which was nothing more than a modified shipping container with an air conditioner. It was shared by the three of them: Gustavo, who fancied himself these days as an evangelist and had the Bible open on his keyboard at his desk, and Geovanny and David, who had their own crude plywood desks with their own computers. Both were hard at it, or at least doing a good job of pretending to. Gustavo held the door open for me and as I walked in they both stood up and nervously greeted me. I broke the ice by greeting both cheerfully and told them how appreciative we all were for the hard work they had done getting the necessary repairs done to restore the park to 100-percent capacity and exceeding all expectations. They were obviously glowing with pride with grins from ear to ear and to finish my chat I informed them that they would be receiving a ten-percent increase to their salaries for performance and cost of living adjustment. They must have wanted to pinch themselves; a visit from the boss, the first ever, to congratulate them and give them a raise, also the first in three years. David looked like he wanted to say something to me, and I looked at him as if to say, "Go on then man, spit it out!" but then he choked and nothing came out.

Outside, Gustavo had a wry grin on his face "Very well done, Chief. Coming over to visit us and leaving behind your mirror."

"How so, Gustavo? What do you mean by that 'leaving behind a mirror'?" I asked.

"Well, very similar to the Conquistadores, buying over the Indians with little mirrors." That lopsided grin of his I didn't know how to interpret, whether it was humour or a subtle dig at my heritage or my somewhat autocratic management style.

I did find his metaphor amusing, but when I drove away I had a feeling of unease that made me shake my head as if I had bitten into a sour lemon. As I looked back into the rearview mirror, he was still standing there watching my car pull away with that sardonic grin on his face, peering over his glasses as if he knew and was relishing my unease.

Oxford Blue

Through a series of coincidences and chance meetings with acquaintances, I became Her Majesty's Honorary Consul for the Islands. More a privilege to serve the Queen I adored and respected than anything else; the pay was a meager stipend that barely covered any expenses. I was given some official-looking business cards and a rubber stamp as well as the old cast iron coat of arms that had once hung in the last official embassy in Tegucigalpa. It was gathering dust in the bodega of the embassy in Guatemala and while attending the Queen's birthday party one year I salvaged it and had a local signmaker restore it to its original colours and glory. It adorned a wall in the front of my office on the main road and when I flew the Union Jack or the flag of St. George it was a sight to behold.

I had my full-time occupation, mind you. I owned a small company with a steady income that allowed me the flexibility to attend the requirements of service that arose occasionally. There was a small community of full-time British citizens, my "patch" as it is referred to in the trade, who mainly kept to themselves and who I never really met often but visited from time to time if I knew they were vulnerable. Actually, they represented a liability if they were to die tragically by suicide or overdose, leaving me with the headache of dealing with the authorities, the next-of-kin, and eventually repatriation. Like all British living in far-flung corners of the diminished Empire as expatriates, they had a stories to tell and colourful ones at that. I knew one who had been an RAF pilot in Korea and spent a year as a POW, another who had played rugby for Gloucester against the Springboks and then made a successful career in the city as a detergents magnate. Most were young, though, and had opted out of society for hedonistic or minimalistic pursuits. I had much in common with them but due to my antipodean accent, fluency in Spanish, and Latin appearance it took a while to convince them of my heritage and it was a struggle to fit in at times since the expatriate groups were very cliquey.

The work was mostly clerical, associated with arranging emergency passports for tourists who had lost theirs or had it stolen. It was mostly a matter of vetting the applicants and crossing their names and passport numbers with a large database stored in a server in Whitehall somewhere that was always crashing, exacerbated by the fact that our third world internet network was in its experimental stages. I had a little office on my property where I had a safe, a filing cabinet, a framed picture of Her Majesty, my Exequatur, and a hand-crafted oak desk behind which I sat in the gloom when I had a "customer" as the FCO insisted they be called.

The paperwork I didn't care much for and when there was a consular case requiring a prison visit, court visit, or deceased citizen I would drop everything else, being more of a field man. Most of these field visits weren't pleasant since they almost entirely involved death or near death and the limits of the human experience. My enthusiasm was driven, I suppose, by a dark, vicarious urge to know more about the decline, fading away, and eventual passing of human life. I think that we all as humans share this curiosity to know what we will eventually face. Most often the next-of-kin, or NOK as they were clinically referred to on reports and other such paperwork, lived back in the UK and hadn't had contact with their deceased relatives for years. It was a macabre feeling standing over an ashen corpse having a conversation with a sister in Sussex who had actually thought their kinfolk were long deceased anyway and asking if they would opt for a pauper's burial at a local graveyard or fork out thousands of pounds for repatriation. A straightforward choice but one that had to be decided, if we went by the book, by the closest relative.

One such Brit in my patch was George, who had made a small fortune in the stock market before retiring from the city and marrying for the third time a woman forty years his junior, a Canadian with an athletic figure, striking blue eyes, and curly blonde hair. Sarah. She was voluptuous with wide hips, full lips, and that knack that some women possess of knowing exactly how to look at a man to give them the feeling that they were desired. He was one of three Brits who lived on the east side of the island, and he seemed to enjoy his life at the new house that they had built on Spyglass Hill. The house had views of both sides of the island and fresh breezes from all sides that kept them cool in summer months. I would pay him a visit occasionally when I was up that side of the island for work and would stop and have a cup of tea with him—he kept a constant supply of PG Tips—and we would chat for a while, mostly listening to his reminiscing or discussing rugby or cricket news from England. We would sit on canvas deck chairs on his wooden deck, looking out to sea, enjoying each other's company. He had been to public school and then up at Oxford where he had earned himself a Blue for rowing and played cricket and rugby for the University and against Cambridge. He had worked his way up and done well in the city, but like most success in the city, it came at a price and he had been divorced twice. I had seen photographs of him as a young man, athletic and strikingly handsome, but the good life of five-course meals and casks of ale and wine with little exercise had taken its toll. He now reminded me of some masters I'd had at school and I saw a bit of my grandpa in him. His florid complexion, bloodshot eyes, and red nose suggested that he had a problem with booze. On one such visit I noticed that he seemed swollen and he complained his gout was playing up. Sarah always seemed distant with me, and I sensed an indifference to George's wellbeing. In fact, most times I visited she was never there, except for one day when I found her sitting next to him, both covered by the same blanket on two separate chairs next to each other.

"George would like to tell you something," she said as she threw off the blanket and slid gracefully into the kitchen to make tea, affording me a wanton gaze as she passed close enough for me to catch a hint of her musky perfume. I suspected that he knew she was too young for him and that she had a wandering eye, but he doted on her and it was one of his pleasures besides Scotch and gin to watch her as she strutted around in front of him or simply lay on the couch with her curls draped over the armrest and her long legs stretched out and crossed with her cotton dress open up to her upper thighs revealing her immaculate white skin. Like any old man with a younger woman, he would turn a blind eye to much just to be able to gaze upon her and notice her every motion day and night. Being as astute as she was, she knew how to keep him enthralled.

"Now look here, young man," as he always addressed me but which in no way I took to be condescending since my old grandad would say the same and it was comforting, "I would like to say how much I enjoy your company and our weekly chats. I'll get to the point, I think I'm ill and Sarah wants me to visit the doctor. I'm not sure what it is but I just feel something's wrong. I'm passing blood, you see, and I suspect it must be the drink."

I wasn't at all surprised. I had noticed his complexion gradually turning yellow even in the two years I had known him. He seemed to realize he was going downhill and went as far as to mention that he wasn't open to returning to the UK, that he would take his chances with local healthcare on the mainland, and that he and Sarah would be off for the following week and would I keep an eye on the house and pop in for a bit each day.

It was handy for me since I was running a project close by and had to go there every day for couple of hours and so I would time it by going a little before lunchtime and taking a sandwich with me. I had a key and after checking on the two aging, snaggle-toothed dogs who always seemed pleased by my presence as well as a quick chat with the gardener, I would let myself in and make a cup of tea. Out on the ample deck, I would sit myself in the chair-swing looking out over the reef in the near distance, enjoying the soothing sight of the bands of blue that denoted the different depths and coral patches around which I could see in my mind's eye the schools of yellow grunt and the random snappers rushing busily seeking out morsels.

On the final day before George and Sarah's return, a Friday, it was looking menacingly dark over the sea to the north. It was flat calm and the darkness of the clouds was punctuated only by jagged spikes of lightning. Seconds later came the rumble of thunder, muffled by many kilometers of heavy air between here and there. It was September, hurricane season, calm, humid, and intolerable at nighttime with the mosquitos. The silence but for the buzz of the cicadas and the darkness of the sky was haunting. George crossed my mind for an instant and I felt a heavy sadness for him and hoped that I would not end up like him in my old age, far away from home waiting for a slow, inevitable, self-inflicted death with a person that I wasn't entirely sure loved him.

I visited the following week and found him in the downstairs garage where he kept his work bench and his tools. He was fairly skilled with his hands, building small gadgets to perform everyday tasks like picking mangos or peeling oranges. He had a plywood trestle table set up in the garage where he had been spray painting the parts for one of his gadgets. He was disassembling his paint gun for cleaning with trembling hands.

"Don't just stand there, give us a hand then will you!" he growled jokingly. I finished disassembling the canister for him and started cleaning it with the strong turpentine thinner. "I have cirrhosis, you know, don't have long now the doctor said, a few months, at best a year. Gave me treatment to slow it down and help with the pain. Suggested I lay off the booze for a bit—ha! Fat chance of that!"

Once again, I wasn't at all surprised. He spent most of his time drinking, although it was never that apparent, but Sarah said he would drink a liter of white rum a day. I knew it had to be his liver by his ever-swelling abdomen and yellowing complexion.

"Will you go back to England?" I asked.

"I'm too feeble to travel now. It would finish me off," he said, feigning stoicism.

We went up on the verandah for our customary tea and sitting to his right, the evening sun was such that it caught the bright blue of his eyes, the same eyes of his youth that once looked out from the pitch as he took to the crease, opening the batting for Stowe. The same eyes that once sparkled as he gazed upon a past love while they went punting in summer on the river in Oxford. He sighed a sigh that sounded like resignation as he recalled some unknown regret or untold secret. I tried to cheer him up by talking about the cricket which always sparked his interest, but he just hummed whimsically. "Hmmm." His mind was wandering, more than likely reminiscing, and I decided to leave him alone. As I left, I held his left hand in both of mine and he squeezed tight, shaking. His eyes welled up, but he never once looked at me as his gaze stayed fixed out to sea towards Cuba. "Goodbye, George," was all I could manage as the lump grew in my throat and I felt my voice break.

A week passed and George was often on my mind. It was a few years before the widespread use of mobile phones and so most calling was done using a landline, which not everyone had the luxury of. I had one of the first mobile phones on the island, a Motorola, with a mouthpiece the size of a wafer that was flipped open to speak after the finger long antennae was extracted. Cumbersome, yet a novelty at the time. George and Sarah had one as well and they and other Brits, who had mobiles, would call if they needed advice or help. I hadn't heard anything from them for a week but didn't want to bother them checking up on George since I considered that I should respect their privacy at this time. Two weeks passed and I had to go to Diamond Rock and would pass their house. I decided to "pop in," as the English say, and say hello.

As I pulled into the drive I was surprised to see three other cars that I recognized as belonging to neighbours from nearby Punta Blanca. It seemed like there must have been a lunch party on or such; when I parked my truck and got out, I heard Sarah's scandalous laugh above the more measured murmuring of the others present. I walked up the front stairs and as I got there noticed that she had a generous glass of red in her hand as did a few of the guests, albeit reluctantly it would seem.

"Oh, hello, Matt," she said, always trying to affect a posh English accent although she was Canadian. "Fancy a glass of wine? No, of course you wouldn't, you don't drink." More laughter as she looked to the others to join in.

"Where's George?" I asked.

"Oh, he's downstairs in the garage."

I excused myself from the group and went down the indoor stairs into the garage, which strangely had been closed when I entered the driveway. Normally, when he was tinkering inside George would have the door open. As I entered the garage the first thing that struck me was the smell of Vicks VapoRub as well as the fact that the light was off, but in the gloom I made out the distinct shape of a body under a bedsheet lying on the plywood trestle table he had made to spray paint on. George was indeed in the garage, but he was deceased.

I struggled to take in the scene with the impromptu drinks party going on upstairs, the fact that no one had notified me (I assumed that he had passed within the past few hours), and the shock of him passing so unexpectedly. I had hoped that he would have a few months of life left at least. As I collected myself, I braced myself and rolled the sheet back from his face to have a last look at him. His eyelids were open and despite the dilated pupils his eyes were the same youthful blue that I had always enjoyed seeing. The broken veins once noticeable on his cheeks and nose in life had disappeared in death. His flesh, not yet ashen for he had just passed, had taken on a peaceful pale ivory hue and he actually looked younger in death than in life. I said goodbye in my mind to him and remembered that I had said goodbye to him a fortnight before and for that I was glad. I then realized that was why I had been overcome by emotion the last time I saw him, for I was not aware it would have been the last time, but my subconsciousness knew. As I turned from the trestle table to leave, Sarah was coming down the stairs with the local doctor and her assistant and bottles and bags which I assumed to be the embalming equipment.

"I shan't expect us to repatriate him, too much money. We'll do a local burial. I'll let you know the dates, maybe you could read something. He was fond of you. Cheerio, Matt."

"Cheerio, Sarah."

The Walnut Box

Rifleman Hewitt threaded his way through the *Haak-en-Steek* thorn trees in what was Northern Ovamboland's flat, dirty sea sand terrain. There were twenty-five of them in a classic V-formation with two bushman trackers and a man and his dog up front. It was the second day of the patrol. He was eighteen and like most of the others in his platoon had received his call up papers during his Matric year and went straight to basics; despite his British citizenship, he had volunteered. A year later he had now been stationed in South West for a month already and this was his first patrol, expected to last between three and five days.

As briefed, they didn't leave through the front gate but went over the wall—berm, really—at the back of the base. Off they went, past the *kakgat* and out into the bush. On this second day they had already walked forty kilometers total and at last light stopped to set up a *TB*. In the *TB* they slept in a large circle with only one entry point. If they had to go to the bathroom they would exit and enter through the same point. At night, everyone was tied to one another with paracord so that when the guard changed you didn't make a sound, just tugged the cord. The boy and his *makkers* copied the bushmen, scraped the top layer of packed sand about six inches into a rough pillow, propped the webbing against it, climbed into the tapered sleeping bag, and tied the drawstring around their necks to keep out the creepy-crawlies. He had learned to bury his water to chill it at night; with the chlorine tablets it tasted awful, but it was better ice cold.

That second night of this, his first patrol, the bushman trackers dug trenches to sleep in with their bare hands because they swore the *terrs* were going to attack. Sure enough, at 0100 they heard the mortar pipes thumping in the near distance. The enemy overshot the patrol because they didn't know exactly where they were. The boys sat *fast* and tried to go back to sleep; the *terrs* knew they were in the area and started walking, looking for them. The boy and his *makkers* didn't hear them and the *terrs* didn't see them either.

Only at first light when they saw the chevron-shaped bootprints did they discover that the *terrs* had walked right through the middle of the *TB*. The bushmen followed the spoor and the patrol ambushed them at mid-morning when spikes, which is what they called the sun, was straight up above pounding down on them while they did their wickedness. It was a short contact; Hewitt and his *makkers* didn't see much happen because they fought from a distance. There were only five enemy. Three were neutralized and two got away. After it was all done, Sparky radioed for the choppers, who came in and extracted the platoon and the dead terrs.

They got back to base at midday, the contact cutting the patrol short and the two bodies that they had brought for ID left in the sun while everyone chowed and got naked to shower at the water tower; some didn't even bother and showered with their browns on. At the end of the day after the *SWATF* had identified and photographed the bodies, Hewitt and other *roefs* were ordered to take them to the *kakgat*. Straight to the *kakgat*, no winning of hearts or minds. They dug three shallow graves and placed the bodies in, no dignity. Some older soldiers were horsing around and making fun of the bodies, putting cigarettes in their mouths, ears, and noses. Although they had been told to place the bodies face down, they were face up in the graves and a barrel of fuel was poured on them and lit. When a body burns the skin goes black, then white, as it burns off. A burning body's muscles contract and often cause it to sit up which is why the troops were told to lay them face down. One of the three bodies sat up and Smit nervously swung a shovel at him in shock, decapitating him. Death was always distant, but burning bodies made death more real, more real to Hewitt than anything he had seen.

2

Jane Stevens, at the precise time a group of young men thousands of miles south were watching as Staff Sergeant Viljoen lowered his Zippo lighter into the shallow graves filled with fuel behind the *kakgat* at Ombalantu Base in South West Africa, was putting the kettle on in her Victorian cottage in Oxfordshire, wondering how on earth to open the walnut trinket box that her mother had bequeathed her after her recent death. She had entertained breaking it open but suspected that the box was just as valuable as its contents. The key to the box was an old skeleton type, and she had searched all of her parents' belongings and turned everything upside down, had even had a locksmith look at it; he could not guarantee the box would not suffer damage.

She considered herself a Christian woman, God-fearing like her parents before her and her sisters. She attended service regularly and participated in church activities, but she also harboured within her a curiosity of the unknown and believed in the perpetuity of the human spirit, although she would never admit this to her church brethren. The missing key remained in the back of her mind and the walnut case on her bedside table almost as if it had life and eyes glaring at her. Beside her husband and her three girls she had two sisters, one of whom had married and lived in South Africa for years and would have no knowledge of the key's whereabouts. The older sister had stopped talking to her after their mother had died and the will was announced. Being the youngest and living closest to her widowed mother it had always fallen upon her to care for her, to run errands, and finally with her husband to make the funeral arrangements upon her passing.

Browsing through the *Henley Standard* on a Monday in the classifieds, an ad caught her eye:

"God gifted Psychic, Sally Dawsan, Solves Impossible problems, Never fails, 100% guaranteed."

Solves impossible problems was what reeled her in; she felt the draw and called the number.

3

Life on the border for Rifleman Hewitt and the rest of Hotel Company took on the mundane, twisted routine of a colonial outpost, like something out of *Beau Geste* as they joked, especially since there were several palm trees surrounding the base. They were stationed at Ombalantu, a sort of army base-cum-squatter-camp outside the Northern Owambo village of Outapi, strategically located in the middle of a wide flat *chana* with two hundred meters of open ground around it in all directions. Surrounding the base was a sand berm (the wall) and in the very center a canteen made of tin; it couldn't really be called a mess hall. Surrounding the canteen were many large square canvas tents where the soldiers slept and relaxed when not on patrol and these were interspersed by lookout towers; there were three companies of infantryman and a contingent of bushman trackers from 101 Battalion and the *doggies*. Off to one side of the base was the HQ tent complex and next to it a large Baobab tree, big enough to drive a Bedford truck through. The tree had been hollowed out over time and the chaplain and perhaps the chaplain before him and a few men had made a small chapel with chairs and a pulpit inside. Angola was ten klicks north of them.

A regular activity was patrolling the long, straight, white road, one of the *lyne*, leading to the base with the engineers and their headsets and detecting wands, walking with great long strides ahead of them looking for mines. The early morning dawn patrol was popular because it meant that whoever participated didn't do guard duty at night and would have some spare time to play cards, listen to music, or *ballas bak*. Hewitt and his squad were returning from one such patrol one morning to find Hotel Company *treeing aan*.

Commandant Baard, a short, wiry man with muscular, hairy forearms was already into his briefing. He was in his element; he loved war and making a nuisance for the enemy. The Company were all sitting down and listening, some munching on chocolate bars, others sipping from water bottles. They listened to this small man's booming voice announcing what they had always dreaded, that the following day at dawn they would cross the border into Angola on a *kaksoek* mission, four platoons. "It is time for us to stop patrolling, waiting to run in to SWAPO. We are going into Angola looking for him."

Not cowardly by any means, Hewitt was thoughtful after listening to the Commandant's briefing about the crossing into Angola. He knew it was inevitable since they were stationed so close to the border. He had heard so many stories about there being Cubans and Russians who used cruel torture techniques on prisoners and even sent some to Siberia to be indoctrinated. A regular churchgoer since childhood until joining up, active member of the youth group and even sat the Scripture Union exams, he had besides all of this a very strong faith in God and in the promise of Jesus's teachings. Ever since he had been on the border he had regularly attended the chaplain's services and prayer meetings which brought him calm and a courage to face his fate. He confessed his sins and commended his earthly life to God so that if he died in the flesh, his spirit would live on.

"To live is Christ and to die is gain," Chaplain Stone always read from Philippians to comfort them.

The evening before the border crossing on the operation, a few attended a short service and prayer meeting with the chaplain in the area around and inside the Baobab tree. The message was from the Gospel of St. Peter, chapter 5, verse 7: "Cast all your anxiety on Him because he cares for you." The peace after the message was tangible and the boys didn't care if they were to die the next day; they were saints. The nail-biting and head-scratching tension made way for laughter and hugs. Someone among the squad had a Kodak camera and had Chaplain take a picture of three riflemen from 1st Squad, Second platoon, including Rifleman David "Dave" Hewitt 84I3456BG in the evening sun, setting on their young faces, all in browns with their bush hats rolled up in their hands and the hollowed-out Baobab chapel in the background.

4

Jane had taken a while to find the semi-detached house in Wallingford, a thirty-minute drive away and despite the unkempt, postage-stamp size front garden and the blue paint peeling off the front door, she rapped the brass bear's paw knocker twice and after a minute heard shuffling inside and a cat's anguished shriek as if a tail had been stood upon. The door was cracked open and only after Jane announced herself to the shrouded character did she unhook the safety chain and bid her to enter. The place wasn't dirty but was particularly untidy; several cats of different breeds and colours were curled up on the stairs and the chairs and a collective, out-of-synch purring was drowning out the classical piece that was playing on the radio in what appeared to be the kitchen.

The hunched figure, who must have been Mrs. Dawsan, didn't introduce herself. She was shrouded in what would seem to be a shawl; despite her apparently advanced age her face was youthful with barely a wrinkle, her eyes a piercing green. A wisp of dark hair had worked its way loose of the shawl to hint that despite her years she wasn't that grey either. It was as if there was a thirty-year-old head on a ninety-year-old body. Jane was at that moment convinced that there was a purpose for her being in that unspecial house at that particular point in time.

"We'll have a cup of tea and a chat then, shall we, my dearest?" the older woman announced as she sat on an intentionally positioned sofa chair to Jane's left. Mrs. Dawsan held Jane's left hand in both her hands and looked at her with the piercing greens as if she were reaching inside of her mind and soul at the same time. Her bony hands were surprisingly warm and fleshy, and Jane felt comforted. "Why are you here, my dearest?"

Jane felt herself pouring her truth out and almost sobbing as she did so. She told Mrs. Dawsan about the box and the key and about her father and recently deceased mother and her sister who lived in South Africa and had three children she had only seen in photographs and whom she knew very little about and her sister and estranged nieces and nephews who lived five miles up the road and didn't speak to. She didn't know why she was so emotional and why she was telling all her truth, but it was cathartic and she felt peace.

"I have a man with me now, an old man, with a long, white beard and long, white hair," Mrs. Dawsan exclaimed out of the silence, her green eyes becoming more vibrant and appearing to search through Jane's eyes into her mind, so much so that her head was shaking slightly from side to side. "He is a tall man, a kind, smiling type... he is dressed in a long, white cassock... he detests the smell of lavender, it bothers him."

Now this whole exchange took thirty to forty-five minutes; there were ten- to fifteen-minute intervals between her words. Mrs. Dawsan was intense and never once leaned back in her chair, her gaze fixed on Jane. Jane suppressed the urge to ask, "But does the man know where the key is?" Mrs. Dawsan's eyes were holding her captive; it was as if she were in one of those dreams when you are laying down and have to get away but for as much as you try, you can't get up.

"The old man is a kind man and is standing behind a boy dressed in brown clothes... his hands are on the boy's shoulders..." Mrs. Dawsan moved her head from one side to the other abruptly, her neck audibly cracking. The Persian cat curled up on the sofa in front of them in the dimly lit room opened its eyes, stopped purring, and went back to sleep.

Not once did Mrs. Dawsan separate her gaze from Jane. "There is a wide tree behind them, a tree with no leaves and hollow inside... there is a cross on a pulpit and chairs... the old man wants to tell you and your closest not to worry about the boy, he will always look after him as he has done since he was born."

And that was the end of it. She broke her gaze, let go of Jane's hand, and slumped into her chair, her eyelids closed. She seemed exhausted.

"Please don't ask me anything else about what I have told you... I don't have the answers... all I know is that the man who spoke through me is connected to you somehow through blood."

Although it was not the information she had been seeking, Jane was indeed intrigued by the whole exchange, although none of it made much sense. She paid the modest fee, in cash, and left Mrs. Dawsan slumped in her armchair stroking one of her cats, her piercing green eyes now just cooling embers of their former selves. On the drive back home, she wondered if it had all been a dream.

5

The night before the beginning of Operation Dolfyn (Dolphin in English) as it was to be called, there was a sense of excitement like Christmas Eve. The tent lights stayed on until late into the night while the men readied their weapons and kits for a long stay in the bush. Before dawn they were taken in a line of *Buffels* to *Oom Willie se pad* and as the sun was breaking pinkish over the horizon they debussed, covering each other and in extended line formation stepping over the rickety barbed wire fence into Angola. They patrolled slowly, forming a V, heavily laden with kit, mortar bombs, ammo, and water. Everyone to a man felt it; they were not alone. Invisible eyes pierced their backs as they advanced. They constantly scanned the bush with a clear vision of what a *terr* looked like now that they had shot them, lurking among the bushes. It was almost disappointing that they didn't encounter any on that first day when they stopped in a small thicket that evening and set up a *TB* for the night. They had covered about twenty klicks that first day of hard humping, loaded down.

They stood watch, two at a time as usual, while the others tried to sleep. Even the night sounds were different in Angola. No one dared sleeping, fearing being shot in their foxholes. The next morning the security patrol rose at daybreak to scout the area before the whole platoon got up and found some chevron-shaped SWAPO boot prints not far from the *TB*. It jittered everybody, and they moved out cautiously at a right angle for a klick to where they were headed to avoid an ambush before heading north again towards a place on the map called Cuvelai. The further north they went in Angola, the less comfortable they felt; they were indeed in someone else's country.

Three days into the op, and every morning the security patrol had found a spoor around the *TB*, sometimes two or three. On the morning of the fourth day there were a dozen separate spoors.

Dave had noticed that Angola smelled differently and the further north they ventured the stronger the smells were. He couldn't quite nail down what the smells were, but they were somehow familiar to him, much as the sound of the turtle dove and the Barbet which accompanied them everywhere and were a constant since he had memory. The smells were herby in a pungent way but with a slight hint of something familiar that took him back to his Granny's place in Rosebank and the lavender-lined flower beds on either side of the steps. Of course, there was none of this in Owamboland, he thought, but there was probably a plant here that gave off the same trace, much like rosemary smells like *Bluegum*.

On that fourth day towards mid-morning, the terrain had begun to change as they headed northwest towards Xangongo. They were careful to skirt the town since intel mentioned that it was heavily garrisoned by Cubans and FAPLA. The platoon was on a high ground overlooking a village on the outskirts of the town; intel was that the village was hiding a weapons cache for SWAPO somewhere therein. Second platoon had been split up into three squads, two stoppers and one attacking; the boy was in the attacking squad. They had hardly begun the descent into the *mahangu* field when a PKM opened up. The PKM is a horrifying weapon with a staggering rate of fire and has a very distinctive sound. It opened up on them from the opposite side of the village and shredded absolutely everything around them. The soldiers couldn't believe that they had hit every tree, bush, and shrub but had somehow missed them. The area smelled like a sawmill and that strange lavender smell came through stronger than ever.

There were leaves and twigs falling all around them, and they were covered in a dusty cloud from the dirt the rounds had kicked up. They had been in the open with no cover whatsoever and everything around them was shot to pieces yet none of the squad had been hit! The mission in the end was successful; they found weapons and explosives in a *grondseil* in the middle of three scattered huts and what they couldn't carry they destroyed with C4 and det cord. C-Company two klicks to their east weren't so fortunate and lost two good men and had a handful of wounded; they couldn't call in helicopters until dark so as to not risk detection. The enemy were in their own country and buried their own dead.

1986

After his two years, Dave and the rest of the 4th Battalion were informed that a state of emergency had been declared and that national service had been extended for three months while they were to be sent to the Townships to quell the violence that had spread through the land. Images of necklace killings were etched in their minds; rumours had circulated through the men that while on patrol sitting on the *Casspirs* they would have to tie themselves to the vehicle in case they were hit with rocks and knocked out. If knocked out and on the ground, the *MK* would necklace them or hack them to pieces before anyone noticed they were missing. The *Swaart gevaar* that every white man in South Africa dreaded was now biting at their ankles; it was only a matter of time before the government gave in or made concessions to avoid total bloodshed. The tension was everywhere.

They were all sent home for a week's leave when they got back to Middleburg from the border, and he knew it was his window to leave that life. He hadn't touched his monthly wages or danger pay while in the operational area—there was nothing to buy up there—and he had a handful of Kruger Rands his late grandad had left him. Only he knew what he was going to do; he was driven and it seemed right. Apartheid seemed so wrong after all these years of believing it to be normal and he couldn't actively defend it. His dad, with whom he was staying, knew nothing nor did he seem to care, just numbing himself against the uncertainty each night with his Scotch. They spoke very little, which suited him fine since the only people he could talk with, he felt, were his brothers in arms. He had dreamed of this leave but now that he was home he missed the camaraderie and the sounds and smells of the bush, the comfort of the chaplain's words and sincere counsel.

He bought the ticket from a pokey little travel agent on Rissik Street in Joeys, the cheapest he could find, transiting through Kinshasha and Madrid. Fortunately, his mum had secured him a UK passport, still valid and to which he was entitled, a few years back, seeing the writing on the wall as she always seemed to have a knack for. She had left a few months earlier, taking his younger brother and sister with her; little did she know that her oldest would soon join them.

He packed light, just a few essentials and some personal possessions and photographs in a brown cardboard suitcase that had African country stickers on it from Zambia and Rhodesia and Mozambique, hangovers of his late grandad's time as a travelling fertilizer salesman. His *staaldak*, browns, boots, and the rest of his uniform remained hung up in the wardrobe as if to give the impression that he would soon return. The only three items he took were his *boshoed*, beret, and belt, which he wore. He turned off the light and left the house at 3:00 a.m. and wouldn't return for twenty-five years.

7.

Nine thousand kilometers away, his mother Laura had been living in England for six months, staying in her mother's old home in Peppard while she found her own. Her days were filled with the care of her two youngest, eleven and thirteen, who were adapting well to school and English village life as adolescents do. She had lived away in Africa for nearly twenty years and found it difficult to adapt herself. The one beacon of light was her sister Jane's visits; she lived fifteen minutes away but they made it a point to see each other every other day at least. It was almost as if they had picked right up where they left off all those years ago. As children they had always been best friends despite the five-year age difference, and their laughter filled the afternoons with brightness even on the rainy days.

One crisp spring day with a hint of green in the surrounding wheat fields, the subject of the walnut box came up. Jane related her desperation of trying to find the key after the idea of forcing the box open was discarded as an option and her trip to Wallingford to meet with the aberrant Mrs. Dawsan was unfruitful. Laura, being older, was visibly disquieted when Jane talked about the "Father Time" like old man who had appeared to the medium with his long, snow-white hair and beard, his loathing of the scent of lavender. Jane would have been too young to remember but Laura had very clear, unforgettable memories of their Grandpa Henry, a wealthy coachbuilder in Reading who was a Methodist layminister from Buckinghamshire. She remembered his kind eyes and the fact that he was always smiling, and she also remembered that months before he passed, he had let his hair and beard grow out and that when she sat on his lap she would run her little fingers through his beard as if she were combing it and he would chuckle with satisfaction. In particular she remembered an incident where she had sewed a small linen pouch with her grandma as a gift with mauve-coloured corduroy and filled it with dried lavender to be placed next to his pillow at night as a sleep aid. The day she was going to give it to him she announced this to her father, who said, "Don't do that, love, whatever you do. He will take sick and not eat for days. The old boy hates the smell of lavender, you know." It stuck in her mind since that day when she was six because she just couldn't imagine anyone not liking lavender.

Both of them were gripped and it was as if their chairs and the verandah table were floating somewhere else and nothing else existed, not even their children noisily playing doctors and nurses in the background. Mrs. Dawsan's old man, the protector, was Henry their grandfather and their burning curiosity to know who the boy in the vision was had completely eclipsed the need to open the antique walnut box and peruse its contents. Could the boy also be their blood or was it another boy in some other part of the world belonging to another family who had been adopted in this spirit world by Grandpa Henry, they both wondered.

Several days later, Laura received an operator call saying it was from her son David. "We have a return call from a Mr. David Hewitt. Will you accept the charges?" Although she thought it was from a Tikki box in Africa she accepted the charges without hesitation, anxious for news from him. But he wasn't in Africa; he was at Heathrow about to catch a cab and then a train to Goring-on-Thames. He had merely wanted to prep her since he knew she hated surprises.

She had had very little contact with him over the past two years and even less when he told her in a heavily censored letter that he was going to the border. A phone call a month, a letter every now and again. A thoughtful boy but not a good scholar, he did just enough to pass and was always being naughty both in primary and high school. He had always been popular because of his talent on the sports field, cricket and rugby. He was missed around the house for his jokes and pranks. When the tension surrounding the political situation became too much, creating a rift between her and her husband, and the quarrels became more frequent, she made the decision to leave. It was gut-wrenching for her to have to leave her boy behind, but he was by then bound by law to serve out his two years. She pleaded with him to follow them when he *klaared out*. The last time she'd seen him was on a pass home after six months on the border. He was much changed, chain smoking Camels without the filter, drinking way too much beer, and most of the time staring off into a distance at things only he could see. His face was creased and he was tanned and skinny; he reminded her of the images she had seen of starving POWs in the Second World War. When she tried to engage in conversation to understand what he was thinking or what was eating at him, he would barely look her in the eye and when he did his eyes were as dark and lifeless as coal. She was intimidated by her own son. She was so overwhelmed by sadness at his distance that she just wanted to give him a hug and she did one day during his pass after she had made him his favourite toasted chicken and mayonnaise sandwiches. But he became tense and shirked away from her embrace and lit another Camel. The last time she had seen him was to drop him off at the station; she had given him a Bible with his name embossed on it with a four-leaf clover pressed inside on the page that opened at 1 Corinthians, chapter 13, the same one he had memorized for his Scripture Union exam as a twelve-year-old. It was his favourite and also her Grandpa Henry's:

"For now we see through a glass, darkly: but then face to face: now I know in part but then shall I know even as also I am known."

His half-smile, almost a smirk, and lifeless eyes looking at her and waving halfheartedly, leaning out of the train window as it pulled away from the station was the last image she would have of him. She felt like she would never know, or want to know, the indescribable horror that had robbed her son of his brightness, and she fought away the panic that this would be the last time she would see her boy. She regretted not having tried to hug him tighter and warm his coldness and she regretted not telling him once more that she loved him and would always love him. He would always be her little boy. She had written him a long letter when she left for England and put some photos inside the envelope of her and the family on their last trip to the sea together. She jotted down her address in England and the phone number. It was the number he called on that day, collect.

8.

A month after his arrival in England, things had become uncomfortable in the house. David tired of his mother's fawning and constant nagging. She continued to treat him as a child even though he had been to war and had to look out for his fellowman. The distance he felt between him and his siblings, mainly because of the age difference, was enormous. He missed his *makkers*, the sounds and smells of the bush, and the comforting purpose of the patrols.

He had arrived in rural England at the beginning of summer and there was a need for labourers to take in the harvest and help with the baling activities associated with wheat straw and hay. He grew excited at the promise of rugged, outdoor physical activity. His Aunt Jane's husband Richard was an agricultural contractor and needed help. Early start and late finish, he was told. The pay wasn't great, but he was given a room and board in their cosy Victorian cottage. He worked with Richard and at times with Chris, a Canadian from Calgary, short and wiry with hairy muscular forearms that reminded him of Commandant Baard. Chris was doing his farrier's apprenticeship at Lord and Lady Silsoe's farm where Richard kept his equipment in exchange for taking in their hay and wheat straw every year. It was pleasing company of three, Chris dipping his snuff and breaking into the occasional cowboy melody out of the blue and teasing both of them, while never taking off his farrier's leather apron, Richard up ahead driving his *Zetor* and pulling the cart behind it, puffing on his Briar pipe packed with Murray's Erinmore mixture that left a pleasing trail of pineapple-scented smoke wafting behind for the two bale carters to breathe in. Dave, of course, stuck to his Camels and had mastered the art of being able to throw bales four layers high with the fag clenched between his teeth.

The work was easy when it was hot with no rain because the bales became light, but with a little rain or a strong dew they became heavy and harder to lift and throw. It was in the days when bales were rectangular and held together by two strands of twine that ran lengthwise. They would have competitions to see who could throw the bales the highest. At lunch they would stop at a shady spot and have ploughman's farm cheese and butter, home-baked bread, chicken, and ham with fresh milk and tea. Dave felt guilty tucking in, knowing that his mates somewhere nine thousand klicks south were tucking into ratpacks or anything they could get their hands on. When they worked on Lord Silsoe's estate, his Lordship would ride out on his chestnut mare and often bring them lunch himself and sit with them as they ate and engage in conversation. A bespectacled, slight man, he seemed to have a constant grin on his face and expressed a genuine interest in people's opinions when he posed questions.

"I understand you're from South Africa, young man," he popped off one day to the boy. "Bloody shambles down there, I can see. You chaps just want to farm and mine gold and the blasted Communists want to cash in on the hard work."

"Yes, your Lordship," he answered, "the country has dark days ahead, indeed, but from what I saw in my short time as a soldier all Africans of all races just want the same as us, to give the best to their families. They just see different means to meet that end. Unfortunately, hate between the peoples will only make a deeper wound that, in the end, will be harder to heal."

Lord Silsoe looked far away over the distant hills, stroking his shaved chin. "Hmmm, yes, interesting perspective." He took a large bite of a Scotch egg.

After finishing a day's work, they would go down to The Crooked Billet and sit in Nobby's smoke-filled front room while he served them pints of Brakspears Mild Ale and spun them yarns, his bright red nose getting ruddier. Dave enjoyed this camaraderie which filled the void of his soldier's life. They never judged him or asked him about his past and although they had an idea that he had been in a dark place, they both sensed that it was something he would rather not talk much about because it brought with it both fear and sadness and the idea that they would never understand. He felt at peace in these yellow, dusty English fields divided by hedges and packed with blackberries, nettles (the dock leaves to ease the sting growing among them), and the occasional startled pheasant that would fly out noisily clucking like a turkey. He was asked to play for the village eleven on Saturdays on their slanted pitch; bowling his right arm medium and useful tail-end batting, he became a popular member of the team and actually enjoyed being out in the English sun with the sound of mowers in the near distance, the wholesome smell of freshly cut grass, and the clink of the Cricket Club's aged china while the village ladies brewed the tea and laid out the cake and sandwiches on the pavilion table awaiting the break at the change of innings.

Once in a while, he would be awoken at night out of a deep sleep and a terrible re-occurring nightmare, a burning body sitting up and being decapitated by a shovel. But in the dream it was always his mother wielding the shovel. Sweating, with muscles taut as the legs of a cheetah ready to leap into a sprint, he would never be able to go back to sleep and would go outside and sit on Jane's bench among the pansies, chrysanthemums, and roses and smoke until dawn while reading his Bible and his scribbled references from Chaplain's Bible studies in the margins which would comfort him from the dread.

9.

One Monday they returned home at 4:00 after a short day, having finished taking in a field of wheat straw for a farm outside Stoke Row, and Dave went up to wash up for supper, which was one of his favourites, Jane's stuffed marrow. There was a smallish brown paper wrapped parcel on his bed with *RSA* stamps on it and Craig's handwriting. Craig was his best mate; they had played rugby against each other in high school but in basics formed a bond forged by mutual interests and similar senses of humour.

He opened the package. It contained three medals he had earned for service in the operational area, one of which was the Southern Africa medal which was awarded if any serviceman spent more than twenty-four hours across the border into Angola, the metal of which was taken from a captured Russian T-72 tank. It had a pleasing relief of a leopard prowling across a savannah with some acacia trees behind it. He ran his forefinger across it, remembering the times he crossed the border and how each time he did he felt he would never come back and that creepy feeling that someone was watching them.

There was also an envelope containing a letter from Craig with news of everyone and heavily censored with a few photos inside. One photo was of him and Craig the day they passed out from basics in Middleburg, arms around each other's shoulders, beaming fresh-faced youth all smiles in crispy new browns. Another photo showed Dave, shirtless, tanned with a fag hanging out of the corner of his mouth holding a MAG machine gun from the hip in typical *grensvegter* pose with a bandolier of bullets around his shoulders and waist. The third was his favourite, the one they took after chapel in the Baobab at Ombalantu the evening before they crossed over the border for the first time. There was a soft light, almost a calming glow, that reflected off the boys' faces, the photo having been taken an hour before dusk. The same cherubic faces that would become tanned and gaunt with distant eyes full of fear by the end of their service. He put the photograph on his bedside table propped up on the lamp, thinking he would buy a frame for it next time he went to the village market.

The following day was an early start. In summertime it got light at 4:00 and Jane was already in the kitchen brewing tea, filling thermoses, and packing the lunches for the day. They were out and on the road in the Landy by 5:00 to Gallowstree Common to take in some hay before the rain made down that was expected by midnight. Jane enjoyed this quiet time in between the men leaving and the girls waking up, sitting on her bench listening to the eager birdsong, watching the squirrels scamper along the branches of the elm tree. At 6:00 as usual she would go up and wake the girls and make up the beds. Dave usually made his own, as he was used to, he said, from boarding school and the army, but she supposed to maintain his privacy.

That day, however, she felt a compulsion to enter his room. The minute she did so, she knew why; on his bedside table was a picture of the tableaux the medium had described with the boys in brown. In the centre of the group was her nephew and in the background was the hollowed tree. Grandpa was not there but there was a glow to the scene that was not created by the sun, and she knew he was there and knew that everything Mrs. Dawsan had spoken now made sense. She felt cold and then a comforting warmth and a slight sweat but most of all joy in the knowledge that those who came before us were not only still with us but here to protect us and love us when we most needed.

She sat on the edge of Dave's bed and wept silently but with happiness and relief that her nephew had been spared his life through whatever perils he had passed and her sister spared a broken heart. She found it hard to resist the urge to drive the five miles to Pat Ansty's fields to see Dave and to tell him what she knew but she waited until evening. Although she knew him very little since he had grown up in Africa, she felt close to him and both she and Richard enjoyed his company and his sense of humour with the only exception that he seemed to shun any displays of affection. On the second day that they had gone out, she felt the urge and she supposed the mothering instinct to give him a hug goodbye as she did with Richard, but he tensed up and barely raised his arms.

After dinner on that day, he was in his room ready to turn in and as she climbed the creaking staircase his door was half open and she saw him sitting on the edge of the bed with the photograph between forefinger and thumb with a sad look on his face, as if he were harnessing some power from it. She knocked and entered, and his head jerked sharply as he was startled,

"I just want to tell you something, Dave, and I tell you with much love and I would ask that you not question me on this." She carefully chose her words so as not to make him feel she had been prying. "You are beloved within our family and much loved and have been cared for by the saints before, now, and as you will be for the rest of your life."

He looked puzzled and opened his mouth as if to speak and then didn't. She sensed that he was realizing something and that events or facts were beginning to fall in to place, much like Mrs. Dawsan's vision did to her that morning. No words were necessary between them at that juncture; they both knew.

10.

Precisely the day after the exchange between aunt and nephew, Jane was hemming Richard's Sunday trousers, for it was the village harvest festival the coming Sunday. She had her old biscuit tin filled with threads and assorted pins and needles out, a trove that she took out and rummaged through at least twice a week. This time as she dipped her fingers into the tin to get out the black thread, her fingertips came across, at the bottom edge, a small black primitive key with emerald thread tied to its bow; its bit resembled a three-toed foot with the middle toe shorter than the others. She had never seen it before and was very certain she had not seen it the last time she opened the tin three days prior.

Of course, she knew what it opened and when she tried it, it made a satisfying click as it was turned and the lid of the walnut box sprang open.

Glossary

Kakgat : long-drop toilet

makkers : mates

terrs: SWAPO/PLAN terrorists independence fighters

TB: Temporary Base (for the night)

SWATF: South West African Territorial Force (reservists)

roefs: new recruits (new guys)

Chana: an open, flat plain surrounded by trees

doggies: a contingent of German Shepherds and handlers

lyne: straight dirt roads crisscrossing South West Africa (Namibia today)

treeing aan: standing at attention

kaksoek: "looking for shit"

SWAPO: South West African Peoples Organization

ballas bak: "ball baking" (sunbathing)

Buffels: armoured personnel carriers

Oom Willie se pad: a dirt road running parallel to the Angolan border

FAPLA: Angolan Peoples Liberation Armed Forces

mahangu: millet

grondseil: groundsheet

Casspirs: armoured fighting vehicles

Swaart gevaar: Black Danger

staaldak: tin helmet

boshoed: bush hat

MK: Umkonto weSizwe, ANC armed wing

Zetor: Czechoslovakian tractor

grensvegter: borderfighter (South African comic book character)

RSA: Republic of South Africa

Made in the USA
Middletown, DE
15 February 2022

61193953R00076